QUOTABLE VICES

VICES

by
Carole McKenzie

MAINSTREAM
PUBLISHING
EDINBURGH AND LONDON

First published in Great Britain in 1995 by
MAINSTREAM PUBLISHING COMPANY
(EDINBURGH) LTD
7 Albany Street
Edinburgh EH1 3UG

ISBN 1 85158 636 9

A catalogue record for this book is available from the
British Library

Typeset in Sabon by Litho Link Ltd, Welshpool, Powys
Printed in Finland by WSOY

For my brothers, Max and Jack

Preface

VICE IS ITS OWN REWARD
Quentin Crisp

For centuries, the seven deadly sins of Envy, Lust,
Gluttony, Anger, Greed, Sloth and Pride have
served as a warning to those who are tempted to
stray, but what exactly constitutes a vice?

The dictionary defines a vice as: a fault, blemish,
bad habit or immoral conduct. What becomes
clear from the wide-ranging and contradictory
remarks, witticisms, denouncements and appraisals
quoted in this amusing and unique collection, is
that something which is seen to be quite harmless
by one is sure to be condemned as a damnable vice
by another.

Take diet, for example; a subject close to the
heart of many. Barbara Cartland sees a healthy
diet to be most important: 'The right diet directs
sexual energy into the parts that matter.' Robert
Redford, who perhaps needs no such direction,
maintains on the other hand: 'Health food may be
good for the conscience, but Oreos taste a hell of a
lot better.'

Just as the definition of 'vice' differs from
person to person, so does the willingness in which
one indulges. Some embrace their vice desperately,
such as Mia Farrow, who recently admitted that
when under stress, she took up smoking: 'I needed
a vice real quick.' Others, like Genghis Khan, are
prepared to tolerate vice, but only in moderation:
'A soldier must not get drunk more than once a
week.'

This collection is categorised alphabetically
including, as well as various vices, places in which
vice is prevalent, such as 'Bawdy House' (the
Houses of Parliament) and 'Hollywood'. After
months of allegations and revelations of
impropriety in the House, Edwina Currie, MP,
gave her view: 'The last few weeks have told me

that one person's sexual perversion is another's preferred sexual practice.'

Although many of the people included in this book hold forth on the more common vices, such as sex, alcohol and gambling, there are still plenty who see vice in rather more unlikely pursuits. Take Noel Coward, for example, observing the game of squash: 'That's not exercise, it's flagellation.'

Whatever your chosen vice, enjoy it, and console yourself with the fact that:

> Some people with great virtues are disagreeable, while others with great vices are delightful.
> *Francois, duc de la Rochefoucauld*

ABORTION

It serves me right for putting all my eggs in one bastard.
Dorothy Parker (1893-1967), US writer and wit on going to hospital for an abortion

ABSTINENCE

Richardson: My dear fellow, I'm afraid you'll have to give up sex for four or five days.
Olivier: What's that got to do with it?
Richardson: Phosphates in the brain. You shot all yours, and it's phosphates that retain the memory.
Ralph Richardson (1902-1983), to Laurence Olivier, when Olivier was wooing Vivien Leigh

Abstinence is a good thing, but it should always be practised in moderation.
Anon

I distrust camels, and anyone else who can go a week without a drink.
Joe E. Lewis (1901-1971), American humorist

Abstainer, n. A weak person who yields to the temptation of denying himself a pleasure.
Ambrose Bierce, *The Devil's Dictionary,* 1911

I was T.T. until prohibition.
Groucho Marx (1895-1977)

I'd hate to be a teetotaller. Imagine getting up in the morning and knowing that's as good as you're going to feel all day.
Dean Martin

I'm only a teetotaller, not a champagne teetotaller.
George Bernard Shaw (1856-1950), Irish dramatist, novelist and critic, *Candida*

The total deprivation of sex produces irritability.
Elizabeth Blackwell (1821-1910), US physician, *The Human Element in Sex*

I am the last person I would fancy if I saw myself at a party. I just assumed people would vomit at the idea of having sex with me anyway.
Stephen Fry, British author and actor, admitting to a 14-year abstinence from sex, 1994

ADULTERY

It [adultery] needs to be considered on a case-by-case, individual-by-individual circumstance – how it affects the individual's job.
Sir Norman Fowler, Tory chairman, announcing that ministers who commit adultery need not always quit, 1994

There are few who would not rather be taken in adultery than in provincialism.
Aldous Huxley, Antic Hay

What men call gallantry, and gods adultery
Is much more common where the climate's sultry.
Lord Byron (1788-1824)

Having a wife, be watchful of thy friend, lest false to thee they fame and goods he spend.
Cato the Elder (234-149BC), Roman statesman

The husband who decides to surprise his wife is often very much surprised himself.
Voltaire (1694-1778)

Adultery is in your heart not only when you look with excessive sexual zeal at a woman who is not your wife, but also if you look in the same manner at your wife.
Pope John Paul II

I say I don't sleep with married men, but what I mean is that I don't sleep with *happily* married men.
Britt Ekland, Swedish film actress

If you should take your wife in adultery, you may with impunity put her to death without a trial; but if you should commit adultery or indecency, she must not presume to lay a finger on you, nor does the law allow it.
Cato the Elder (234-149BC), Roman statesman, on the dowry

If the husband is the criminal, he escapes with little or no injury either to fame or fortune. If the wife is the criminal, the persecutions of the world and her incapacity to make honourable provision for herself, compel her to join the ranks of prostitutes.
T. Bell, British doctor, *Kalogynomia,* 1821

An interviewer asked me what book I thought best represented the modern American woman. All I could think of to answer was: *Madame Bovary.*
Mary McCarthy (1912-1989), US novelist, *On the Contrary,* 1962

Segregation is the adultery of an illicit intercourse between injustice and immorality.
Martin Luther King (1929-1968), American black leader

The minute you start fiddling around outside the ideas of monogamy, nothing satisfies anymore.
Richard Burton (1925-1984)

I've never been out with a married woman, never. I respect others' properties.
Michael Caine, Look, 1967

I enjoyed being an adultress . . . taking a certain vengeance of the fact that my husband was not being faithful.
Joan Collins

It's a game I never play.
Sophia Loren, 1964

Monogamy is impossible these days for both sexes. I don't know anyone who's faithful or wants to be.
Goldie Hawn, 1977

I couldn't stand that my husband was unfaithful. I am Raquel Welch – understand?
Raquel Welch, 1973

Adolescence: a stage between infancy and adultery.
Anon

ADVICE

Never eat at a place called Mom's. Never play cards with a man named Doc. And never lay down with a woman who's got more troubles than you.
Nelson Algren, *What Every Young Man Should Know*

The strongest possible piece of advice I would give to any young woman is: Don't screw around, and don't smoke.
Edwina Currie, MP

AFFAIRS

I haven't had as many affairs as Joan Crawford – but outside of a cat house, who has?
Bette Davis, American actress

What I have seen of the love affairs of other people has not led me to regret the deficiency in my experience.
George Bernard Shaw

I do not see the EEC as a great love affair. It is more like nine middle-aged couples with failing marriages meeting at a Brussels hotel for a group grope.
Kenneth Tynan, 1975

I don't remember any love affairs. One must keep love affairs quiet.
The Duchess of Windsor

I shouldn't have had an affair. On the Richter Scale, this may not be a grave thing for anyone else. But for me it's the most awful thing in my whole life.
Hartley Booth, MP, speaking of his affair with his research assistant

As far as I know Michael hasn't had an affair, but couples can sometimes sort these things out. Being unfaithful isn't an unbreakable rule between us.
Lizzie Power, actress, four months before her presenter husband, Michael Aspel, made public his affair

I knew about the affair . . . I told Paddy . . . 'look kiddo, you've got to come clean or people will think that it's something much worse'.
Jane Ashdown, on her husband Paddy Ashdown MP's affair

Just how difficult it is to write a biography can be reckoned by anybody who sits down and considers just how many people know the real truth about his or her love affairs.
Rebecca West (1892-1983), British journalist and novelist

I was naïve – I ignored all the warning signs.
Mia Farrow, American actress, after the revelations of Woody Allen's affair with his step-daughter, 1994

Why have hamburger out when you've got steak at home? That doesn't always mean it's tender.
Paul Newman

A G E

The Grecian ladies counted their age from their marriage, not their birth.
Homer

The young have aspirations that never come to pass, the old have reminiscences of what never happened.
Saki (H. H. Munro)

It is a terrible thing for an old woman to outlive her dogs.
Tennessee Williams, Camina Real

There are so many ways of us dying it's astonishing any of us choose old age.
Beryl Bainbridge

Whatever poet, orator, or sage may say of it, old age is still old age.
Henry Wadsworth Longfellow

To some extent I am just an ageing hippie but I pre-date the hippie era, I'm actually an old Fifties adolescent. I've never managed to grow up particularly – I would say I'm the victim of an arrested development.
Richard O'Brien, British actor, writer and presenter

I have my 87th birthday coming up and people ask what I'd most appreciate getting. I'll tell you: a paternity suit.
George Burns, American comedian

You only have to survive in England and all is forgiven you . . . if you can eat a boiled egg at ninety in England they think you deserve a Nobel Prize.
Alan Bennett

You know you're getting old when the candles cost more than the cake.
Bob Hope

I'd like to grow very old as slowly as possible.
Irene Mayer Selznick (1907-1990), stage producer

It is sad to grow old but nice to ripen.
Brigitte Bardot

I was brought up to respect my elders and now I don't have to respect *anybody.*
George Burns at 87

When I started in films, they used to sign on girls for a seven-year contract at 17 or so, because studio doctors and people who were supposed to know thought women had passed their peak at the age of 26.
Joan Collins at 53

An actress I knew – when I filmed with her, I was 31 and she was 36. Today, I'm 40 and she's still only 37.
Tony Curtis, 1965

Females get hired along procreative lines. After 40, we're kind of cooked.
Carrie Fisher, *Time,* 1991

When you're my age, you just never risk being ill – because then everyone says: 'Oh, he's done for.'
Sir John Gielgud at 84

I absolutely refuse to reveal my age. What am I – a car?
Cyndi Lauper, American singer and actress

I'm in pretty good shape for the shape I'm in.
Mickey Rooney at 58

No one is 22. I've got shoes older than that.
Sylvester Stallone, *Rolling Stone,* 1985

Professionally, I have no age.
Kathleen Turner, *Newsweek,* 1989

AGGRESSION

To knock a thing down, especially if it is cocked at an arrogant angle, is a deep delight to the blood.
George Santayana (1863-1892), French writer, critic and scholar

Attack is the reaction; I never think I have hit hard unless it rebounds.
Dr Samuel Johnson (1709-1784)

The great thing about a cab is you can drive more aggressively – you can nose out into traffic jams and people let you in.
Stephen Fry, British author and actor, stating the benefits of owning a black cab

AIDS

I was expecting that call from Liz Taylor.
Holly Johnson, singer, explaining in interview that many acquaintances have slunk back into the shadows, reluctant to befriend someone with AIDS

My message to the businessmen of this country when they go abroad on business is that there is one thing above all they can take with them to stop them catching AIDS, and that is the wife.
Edwina Currie, British politician, 1987

Every time you sleep with a boy you sleep with all his old girlfriends.
Government-sponsored AIDS advertisement, 1987

It could be said that the AIDS pandemic is a classic own-goal scored by the human race against itself.
Princess Anne, The Princess Royal

The most frightening fact about AIDS is that it can be spread by normal sex between men and women. This is still rare in Scotland.
Scottish Sunday Mail

It speeds up your agenda in life.
Holly Johnson, singer, when asked what effect being HIV positive had on him

More people have been to the moon than have caught HIV from a health care professional.
Jim Johnston, surgeon

I would be very surprised if there are not minor episodes of needle sharing in every prison in Scotland.
Les McBain, Governor of Glenochil prison, speaking about the spread of HIV

As a tribute to Freddie Mercury, the concert could scarcely have been more complimentary, but as an attempt to promote AIDS awareness it made about as much sense as an animal rights convention in a knacker's yard.
Toby Young, journalist and critic, of *The Freddie Mercury Memorial Concert,* 1992

People have had to change their behaviour because of AIDS – and about time too.
Barbara Cartland

ALCOHOL

Alcohol may pick you up a little bit, but it sure lets you down in a hurry.
Betty Ford

Alcoholism isn't a spectator sport. Eventually the whole family gets to play.
Joyce Rebeta-Burditt, The Cracker Factory, 1977

An alcoholic is someone you don't like who drinks as much as you do.
Dylan Thomas (attrib.)

Alcohol's very fattening . . . I was, like, a teenager growing up, constantly battling with my weight and I never thought that it might be that – you know, it could be the drink that was doing it. I always assumed it was the food.
Kim Wilde, pop singer

Alcohol is in some ways worse than drug addiction, because once you're out of the drug scene you're out of it but alcohol is always around you, so therefore you have to sort of temper your way of life; you have to look to re-organise your life so that you steer yourself as far away from the temptation of alcohol as you can, because I still get tempted – I mean, there are still days when I'd love to have a pint.
Jimmy Greaves, footballer and television sports presenter

A L I M O N Y

The high cost of leaving.
Anon

She cried – and the judge wiped her tears with my chequebook.
Tommy Manville, 13-times divorced American millionaire

You never realise how short a month is until you pay alimony.
John Barrymore

Alimony: bounty after the mutiny.
Johnny Carson

Alimony – the ransom that the happy pay to the devil.
H. L. Mencken, A Book of Burlesques, 1920

If the income tax is the price we have to pay to keep the government on its feet, alimony is the price we have to pay for sweeping a woman off hers.
Groucho Marx (1895-1977)

Zsa Zsa Gabor is an expert housekeeper. Every time she gets divorced, she keeps the house.
Henny Youngman, American comedian

ALTRUISM

Such a good friend that she will throw all her acquaintances into the water for the pleasure of fishing them out again.
Charles, Count Talleyrand (1784-1838), French statesman, of Madame de Stael

AMORALITY

If he does really think that there is no distinction between virtue and vice, why, Sir, when he leaves our houses let us count our spoons.
Dr Samuel Johnson (1709-1784)

It is safer to be moderately base – to be flexible in shame, and to be always ready for what is generous, good and just, when anything is to be gained by virtue.
Sydney Smith (1771-1845), English writer, clergyman

It's a fact which cannot be swept under the carpet that incidents of sexual innuendo and harassment are commonplace. The policy of women at sea has sadly taken a dive.
Senior Navy Commander, following a report by sociologists revealing sailors are hostile, some even sexist, to women in the navy, 1994

ANGER

Anger is a kind of temporary madness.
Saint Basil (330-379)

No man can think clearly when his fists are clenched.
George Jean Nathan (1882-1958), American critic

There is no fury like an ex-wife searching for a new lover.
Cyril Connolly (1903-1974), British journalist, *The Unquiet Grave,* 1944

Anger repressed can poison a relationship as surely as the cruelest words.
Joyce Brothers, US psychologist and journalist

APATHY

Science may have found a cure for most evils; but it has found no remedy for the worst of them all – the apathy of human beings.
Helen Keller (1880-1968)

The difference between our decadence and the Russians' is that while theirs is brutal, ours is apathetic.
James Thurber (1894-1961), American humorist and illustrator

ARROGANCE

How haughtily he cocks his nose,
To tell what every schoolboy knows.
Jonathan Swift (1667-1745)

The arrogance of age must submit to be taught by youth.
Edmund Burke (1729-1797), Irish philosopher, statesman

Nobody can be so amusingly arrogant as a young man who has just discovered an old idea and thinks it is his own.
Sydney J. Harris, American journalist

ASSASSINATION

My family has learned a very cruel lesson of both history and fate.
Senator Edward Kennedy

Assassination is the extreme form of censorship.
George Bernard Shaw (1856-1950)

The American public would forgive me anything except running off with Eddie Fisher.
Jacqueline Kennedy Onassis (1929-1994), after the assassination of her husband

BACK TO BASICS

Of course it is about good standards and good values. What it is not about is a witch-hunt against individual transgressions.
John Major, defending his 'back to basics' programme

I'll tell you exactly what 'back to basics' means. It's that wonderful combination – champagne, shooting and conservation. If we had a bit more of those and a bit less of the other, we'd all be in better shape.
Nicholas Soames, MP, food minister

Certain things ought to be swept under the carpet. This is especially true nowadays, when people's sexual lives are no longer controlled by old-fashioned morality.
Norman Stone, Professor of Modern History at Oxford, following revelations of Parliamentary scandals

Brazilian President gets down to basics.
Independent – International, 1994, referring to President Itamar Franco in trouble for cavorting at the carnival with a woman who was clearly not wearing knickers

Will the Government install bicycle sheds at Westminster so ministers can get back to basics in relative privacy?
Letter to *The Times*

BAWDY HOUSE

In this place, Margaret Thatcher was not only Mother Courage but the Love Goddess. Alan Clark was not the only one to flirt outrageously with her; even though she responded by giving her suitors a bit of intellectual S & M.
Teresa Gorman, speaking of activities at Westminster, 1994

Of course they have. I've never actually seen it, but if I were talking to the *Sun* I might say I'd heard grunting noises. There are stories about women colleagues glimpsed in the act.
Edwina Currie, MP, when asked if anyone ever had sex in the Palace of Westminster

In Parliament many marriages are going wrong due to the terrible hours they are having to work. It's a big destroyer of the family life . . . It is not just me. All the wives are complaining. We never see our husbands. We do not know where they are most of the time. Things happen.
Mrs Ashby, wife of David Ashby, MP

Was this not the island of Squidgy, Fergie, Carlo and Camilla, where one in two marriages finishes on the rocks, and where nearly one in three children is illegitimate?
La Stampa, Turin, reporting on the moral crisis of British government

In France, Tim Yeo would have been dining out on the town for having a child by such a pretty lawyer. But in Albion, nothing can resist the swelling tide of puritanism mixed with hypocrisy. Our two countries are so close, yet still so distant from one another.
Le Monde, France

All the newspapers have got several journalists assigned full-time going through files, going through every rumour they have ever heard, looking for some scandal. I am amazed they have found so few. There are 650 MPs and they have found half a dozen improprieties.
Peter Lilley, MP, Social Security Secretary

British scandals jeopardising party's back to basics effort.
New York Times headline

Britain is in the midst of an avalanche of scandal. Revelations have ranged from the grimly tragic to the farcical. When Tory ministers began falling out of other people's beds at an alarming rate, the public's revenge was swift and sweet.
Sun Herald, a Sydney-based Sunday tabloid

This place is a ridiculous madhouse seemingly invented by Kafka. You start work at two thirty in the afternoon and you finish at ten at night. It is an institution deliberately designed to give MPs the earliest possible heart attack, to deny them any social life and to smash up their marriages.
Paddy Ashdown, Liberal Party leader, speaking of the House of Commons and its effect on politicians

There has been a lot of sleaze in Britain.
Dennis Skinner, MP

What he [the politician] enters is a hothouse of intrigue and gossip. Although it's true that 600 of our MPs are men, far more women work here, tucked away in offices and libraries, making the place hum with sexual frisson for the men.
Teresa Gorman, MP

BED

She couldn't take it with her when she left, because it was nailed to the floor.
Friend of Lindi St. Clair, Miss Whiplash, speaking of Miss Whiplash's brown suede rotating bed, 1994

For I've been born and I've been wed –
All of man's peril comes of bed.
C. H. Webb (1834-1905), American journalist

Lying in bed would be an altogether perfect and supreme experience if only one had a coloured pencil long enough to draw on the ceiling.
G. K. Chesterton, On Lying in Bed, 1910

Politics makes estranged bedfellows.
Goodman Ace, American writer

Horizontal, I'm fantastic – I can vouch for that and supply the names of other people who'll vouch for it. Jennifer Saunders being one of them. She can also vouch for the fact that I'm a great snogger, because I have to snog her every night in *Mamie O'Rourke,* a play we're in. Sadly it finishes next week.
Dawn French, British actress and comedienne, when asked what she was like in bed

The happiest part of a man's life is what he passes
lying awake in bed in the morning.
Dr Samuel Johnson

Well, if there's anyone who knows what men like
to see women sleep in, it would be you.
Joan Rivers, American chat-show host to Heidi Fleiss,
the alleged Hollywood madam who is launching a new line
in sexy nightwear

David Ashby brought this surfeit of gossip to high
farce by sharing a queen-size bed with a male
friend to save money. I am all for doing things on
the cheap, but the verdict in the tea-room was that
frankly, if he couldn't afford a separate room on
£30,000 a year, we would have had a whip-round
for him.
Teresa Gorman, MP, speaking of recent scandals
involving Members of Parliament, 1994

I have always found going to bed a necessary evil
that interrupts the general flow of things rather. To
go to bed to sleep that is.
Peter Bowles, British actor

Never to bed mad. Stay up and fight.
Phyllis Diller, American comedienne

The cool kindliness of sheets, that
          soon Smooth away trouble and the rough
          male kiss Of blankets.
Rupert Brooke (1887-1915), British poet

It was such a lovely day, I thought it was a pity to
get up.
W. Somerset Maugham, Our Betters, 1923

A few days on your feet and we'll soon have you
back in bed.
Christine Keeler, quoting her doctor

I have known couples stay up till three in the
morning, each hoping that the other would finally
give in and make the bed.
Katherine Whitehorn, British writer and journalist

'Bed,' as the Italian proverb succinctly puts it, 'is the poor man's opera.'
Aldous Huxley, *Heaven and Hell*

Before you take a girl to bed these days you have to have a medical discussion about the plague. So I don't bother much.
Jack Nicholson

Being good in bed means I'm propped up with pillows and my mom brings me soup.
Brooke Shields

BESTIALITY

When someone behaves like a beast, he says: 'After all, one is only human.' But when he is treated like a beast, he says: 'After all, one is human.'
Karl Kraus (1874-1936), Austrian poet and journalist

BILLS

It is only by not paying one's bills that one can hope to live in the memory of the commercial classes.
Oscar Wilde (1854-1900)

Alas! how deeply painful is all payment.
Lord Byron (1788-1824)

BISEXUALITY

I can't understand why more people aren't bisexual. It would double your chances for a date on Saturday night.
Woody Allen

Bisexuality is not so much a cop-out as a fearful compromise.
Jill Johnston, *Lesbian Nation*, 1973

I'm not bisexual but I wouldn't mind if I was because I'd have twice as many people to go to bed with. We might well be doing it with machines soon.
Gary Numan, British pop star

BLASPHEMY

All the faces here this evening seem to be bloody Poms.
Prince Charles, at Australia Day dinner, 1973

A vicious bastard.
Peter Lawford, actor, expressing his opinion of Pal (alias Lassie)

We don't want three more of the bastards out there spreading poison.
John Major, explaining why he did not sack Euro-sceptic ministers, 1993

He spoke the truth. He should not apologise.
Sir Edward Heath, on John Major's 'bastards' comment

Under certain circumstances, profanity provides a
relief denied even to prayer.
Mark Twain (1835-1910)

It is part of free speech to say that a politician has
shown by his statements or his actions that he is
barmy.
Mr Justice Drake, blocking a former Labour councillor's
libel action against a Tory MP

No one is ever capable of swearing properly in any
language other than their own.
Ben Elton, writer and comedian

Nowadays you can't be filthy unless you've got a
degree.
Sir Frankie Howerd, British comedian (1922-1992),
BBC television, *That Was the Week That Was,* 1963

B L O O D Y - M I N D E D N E S S

Some folks are so contrary that if they fell in a
river, they'd insist on floating upstream.
Josh Billings

Why be disagreeable when with a little effort you
can be impossible.
Douglas Woodruff (1897-1978), British journalist and
author

A state of mind halfway between anger and
cruelty.
Wayland Young, British politician and writer

Well, if I called the wrong number why did you
answer the phone?
James Thurber (1894-1961), American humorist and
illustrator

Kirk would be the first to tell you that he's a
difficult man. I would be the second.
Burt Lancaster, on actor Kirk Douglas

BLONDES

Blondes have the hottest kisses. Red-heads are fair-to-middling torrid, and brunettes are the frigidest of all. It's something to do with hormones, no doubt.
Ronald Reagan

Is it possible that blondes also prefer gentlemen?
Mamie Van Doren, American actress

She was a blonde. A blonde to make a bishop kick a hole in a stained-glass window.
Raymond Chandler (1888-1959), American novelist
Farewell, My Lovely, 1940

Who can resist a date with a blonde? She always wanted me to come back. By God I've been lucky haven't I?
Professor Sir Alan Walters on his appointment as economics advisor to Margaret Thatcher

BOASTS

When you're as great as I am it's hard to be humble.
Muhammad Ali, American boxer and world heavyweight champion (attrib.)

There's been three big phases of my celebrity, if you like. With the Boomtown Rats it was Bob the Gob, then with the Live Aid thing it was Bob the God, then it settled down to a general omnipresence.
Bob Geldof, musician

If only I had a little humility, I would be perfect.
Ted Turner (attrib.)

THE BOMB

. . . the French are going the Americans one better with their Michelin bomb: it destroys only restaurants under four stars.
Robin Williams

The survivors of nuclear attack would envy the
dead.
Nikita Khrushchev

If the Third World War is fought with nuclear
weapons, the Fourth will be fought with bows and
arrows.
Lord Mountbatten

If a single NATO bomb strikes a Serbian position,
there will be no more talks.
Radovan Karadzic, Bosnian Serb leader

BORES

A healthy male adult bore consumes each year one
and half times his own weight in other people's
patience.
John Updike, American writer

If you are a bore, strive to be a rascal also so that
you may not discredit virtue.
George Bernard Shaw

A bore is a man who spends so much time talking
about himself that you can't talk about yourself.
Melville D. Landon (1839-1910), American lecturer
and wit

I think people see me as a boring old fart who
should just shut up and go away.
Eric Clapton, British musician

I remember when pop music meant jerking off to
pictures of Marc Bolan and duffing up Bay City
Rollers' fans in lunch breaks. Being 13 was never
as vapid as this. If it had been, we would all be
traffic wardens by now.
Melody Maker, of pop group, *Bros*

The black male dancers in *Hot Gossip* have always
been dead bores, mainly because of the humourless
frowns of concentration while making movements
with their hips which suggest a doomed no-hands
attempt to scratch their groins against an invisible
tree.
Clive James, describing the dance group, *Hot Gossip*

BREASTS

A vacuum with nipples.
Otto Preminger, American film director, on Marilyn Monroe

If anything happens to me, please arrange for me to be buried topless.
Mother of actor George Hamilton, after she revealed that, at the age of seventy-three, she had just had her breasts enlarged by silicone implant

I just won't go back. They don't want to know about my career – they're obsessed with my tits.
Amanda De Cadenet, presenter and model, reflecting on Britain

My bust was visible under the négligé in one scene. Suddenly, there were Barbra Streisand's breasts and I was worried that people might concentrate on my body instead of my acting.
Barbra Streisand, on seeing rushes of the sex scenes with Nick Nolte in the film *The Prince of Tides*

Of course I flaunt my assets. They are big, but I've always had 'em, pushed 'em up, whacked 'em around. Why not make fun when I've earned a fortune with 'em.
Dolly Parton, actress and singer

Miss World has always had its fair share of knockers.
Julia Morley, organiser of the Miss World Contest

Even today, every time I open a magazine I get depressed looking at cleavages which look as if they should be offering day trips. If it wasn't for men's infantile obsessions with large breasts, women wouldn't experience these humiliating scenarios in the first place.
Jaci Stephen, British columnist

It's like saying that the size of a man's gut affects his success.
Libby Purves, when asked 'Is big bad?'

If a woman wears a Wonderbra in the boardroom she's not going to let anyone stand in the way of her career.
A spokeswoman for the *Playtex Wonderbra*

There are two good reasons why men go to see her. Those are enough.
Howard Hughes (1905-1976), of Jane Russell

Dramatic art in her opinion is knowing how to fill a sweater.
Bette Davis, of Jayne Mansfield

Miss United Dairies herself.
David Niven, of Jayne Mansfield

Uncorsetted, her friendly bust
Gives promise of pneumatic bliss.
T. S. Eliot (1888-1965)

When I look back, the fondest memory I have is not really of the Goons. It is of a girl called Julia with enormous breasts.
Spike Milligan, British actor and humourist, celebrating his 75th birthday

B U T T O C K S

A politician is an arse upon which everyone has sat except a man.
e. e. cummings (1894-1962), US poet, *A Politician*

Chevy Chase couldn't ad-lib a fart after a baked bean dinner.
Johnny Carson, American television personality

C A N N I B A L I S M

A cannibal is a guy who goes into a restaurant and orders the waiter.
Jack Benny (1894-1974), American comedian (attrib.)

I came across a tribe of cannibals who'd been converted by Roman Catholic missionaries. Now, on Friday, they only eat fishermen.
Max Kauffmann, American writer and wit

CELIBACY

It takes a lot off your mind, being celibate.
Sex does occupy such a lot of space. I have much
more time now.
Keith Waterhouse, writer and journalist

The only bit of sausage I get is a hot-dog.
John Bobbitt, whose wife hacked off his manhood with a
carving knife

I'm getting hundreds of marriage proposals
through the post. Whenever I make a personal
appearance I get gorgeous girls offering to take me
home. They all want to be the one who gets it
going again.
John Bobbitt

I haven't slid my body over anyone else's for over
ten years.
Stephen Fry, actor and comedian

CENSORSHIP

If a man is pictured chopping off a woman's
breast, it only gets an 'R' rating; if, God forbid, a
man is pictured kissing a woman's breast, it gets
an 'X' rating. Why is violence more acceptable
than tenderness?
Sally Struthers, American writer

Art made tongue-tied by authority.
William Shakespeare (1564-1616)

The main trouble with the censors is that they
start worrying if a girl has a cleavage. They ought
to start worrying if she hasn't any.
Marilyn Monroe

There is more censorship in England than there is
in Spain.
David Hockney, artist

Censorship feeds the dirty mind more than the
four letter word itself.
Dick Cavett, American talk-show host

They can't censor the gleam in my eye.
Charles Laughton (1899-1962), British actor

It is the personification of permissiveness, corruption and perversion of Zimbabwean culture.
Zimbabwe local Government minister,
1965 when a larger than life cast iron statue of a naked man was removed from the Bulawayo City Gardens

I believe in censorship. After all, I made a fortune out of it.
Mae West (1892-1980)

Censorship is the commonest social blasphemy because it is mostly concealed, built into us by indolence, self-interest, and cowardice.
John Osborne, British playwright

They who have put out the people's eyes reproach them of their blindness.
John Milton (1608-1674)

C H A S T I T Y

. . . that melancholy sexual perversion known as continence.
Aldous Huxley, *Antic Hay,* 1923

Only the English and Americans are improper. East of Suez everyone wants a virgin.
Barbara Cartland, British author

A chaste woman ought not to dye her hair yellow.
Menander (342-291BC), Greek playwright

An unattempted woman cannot boast of her chastity.
Michel de Montaigne (1533-1592), French essayist

Your old virginity is like one of our French withered pears; it looks ill, it eats drily.
Parolles, *All's Well That Ends Well.*
William Shakespeare

A woman's chastity consists, like an onion, of a series of coats.
Nathaniel Hawthorne (1804-1864), American novelist

There are a few virtuous women who are not
bored with their trade.
Francois, duc de La Rochefoucauld (1613-1680),
French writer and moralist

These, it is true, are abstinent; but from all that
they do the bitch of sensuality looks out with
envious eyes.
Friedrich Nietzsche (1844-1900)

CHILDISH BEHAVIOUR

Kids learn more from example than anything you
say. I'm convinced they learn very early not to hear
anything you say, but watch what you do.
Jane Pauley, American journalist

A child of one can be taught not to do certain
things such as touch a hot stove, turn on the gas,
pull lamps off their tables by their cords, or wake
mommy before noon.
Joan Rivers

The way to keep children at home is to make
home a pleasant atmosphere – and to let the air
out of the tires.
Dorothy Parker

[Being a parent] is tough. If you just want a
wonderful little creature to love, you can get a
puppy.
Barbara Walters, American journalist

CHOCOLATE

She regarded food simply as fuel, but she's the only
person I've seen eat an entire box of Elizabeth
Shaw mint crisps . . . quite a feat.
Carol Thatcher, of her mother Margaret Thatcher

That's easy. Chocolate. I just love the stuff.
Dawn French, actress and comedienne, when asked:
'What one luxury couldn't you live without?'

Since I gave up men, wine, gambling and snogging behind the bike sheds, my vice has to be preferring white Belgian chocolates to conjugal sex.
Vanessa Feltz, writer and broadcaster

I could understand if 'Piss Flowers' was controversial but not the chocolate fountain.
Helen Chadwick, artist, on her new work, described as a 'cacao phallus girded by glutinous bubbles'

CLASS

I don't believe in class differences, but luckily my butler disagrees with me.
Marc, cartoon, *The Times*

As usual, I have against me the bourgeois, the officers and the diplomatists, and for me only the people who take the Metro.
Charles de Gaulle

The terrifying characteristic of British society is that many of those who are supposed to be inferior have been brainwashed into believing that they actually are.
Tony Benn, British Labour politician

The classes that wash most are those that work least.
G. K. Chesterton (1874-1936)

I don't give a tuppenny hoot.
John Major, when asked about his attitude to class

We can't have anyone too common looking. It would upset my children.
Barbara Cartland, British romantic novelist, describing the actress to play her in a film about her life

CLICHÉS

Man is a creature who lives not upon bread alone, but principally by catchwords.
Robert Louis Stevenson (1850-1894)

If you have to be in a soap opera, try not to get
the worst role.
Boy George

A good catchword can obscure analysis for fifty
years.
Wendell L. Wilkie (1892-1944), American lawyer,
businessman and politician

COCKTAIL PARTIES

The cocktail party – as the name itself indicates –
was originally invented by dogs. They are simply
bottom-sniffings raised to the rank of formal
ceremonies.
Lawrence Durrell, British writer

We are persons of quality, I assure you, and
women of fashion, and come to see and to be seen.
Ben Jonson (1573-1637)

It was one of those parties where you cough twice
before you speak and then decide not to say it
after all.
P. G. Wodehouse (1881-1975), British writer

COCKTAILS

That faint but sensitive enteric expectancy that
suggests the desirability of a cocktail.
Christopher Morley (1890-1957), American novelist
and journalist

I must get out of these wet clothes and into a dry
Martini.
Alexander Woollcott (1887-1943), American columnist
and critic

Cocktails have all the disagreeability without the
utility of a disinfectant.
Shane Leslie

COFFEE

Black as hell, strong as death, sweet as love.
Turkish proverb

Coffee, which makes the politician wise,
And see through all things with his half-shut eyes.
Alexander Pope (1688-1744)

The morning cup of coffee has an exhilaration
about it which the cheering influence of the
afternoon or evening cup of tea cannot be
expected to reproduce.
Dr Oliver Wendell Holmes (1809-1894), American
writer and physician

Coffee in England is just toasted milk.
Christopher Fry, British playwright

COMMITTEES

The English way is a committee – we are born
with a belief in a green cloth, clean pens and
twelve men with grey hair.
Walter Bagehot (1826-1877), English economist and
critic

The heaping together of paintings by Old Masters
in museums is a catastrophe; likewise, a collection
of a hundred Great Brains makes one big fathead.
Carl Jung (1875-1961)

A camel looks like a horse that was planned by a
committee.
Vogue, 1958

Committee – a group of men who keep minutes
and waste hours.
Milton Berle, American humourist

CONTRACEPTION

My husband and I have discovered a foolproof method of birth control. An hour with the kids before bedtime.
Roseanne Arnold, American actress, 1994

I want to tell you a terrific story about oral contraception. I asked this girl to sleep with me and she said 'no'.
Woody Allen

So called 'safe sex', which is touted by the civilisation of technology, is actually, in view of the overall requirements of the person, radically not safe, indeed it is extremely dangerous.
Pope John Paul II

Vasectomies and condoms are as safe for women as anything based on men's behaviour can be.
Spare Rib magazine

The best contraceptive is a glass of cold water: not before or after, but instead.
Pakistani delegate at the International Planned Parenthood Conference

Contraception should be used on every conceivable occasion.
Spike Milligan, British comic actor and author, *The Last Goon Show of All*

The pill came to market and changed the sexual and real estate habits of millions: motel chains were created to serve them.
Herbert Gold, American writer and critic, 1972

Even if the condom in your purse was approaching the sell by date, it would still be worth having it.
Ben Elton, British writer and comedian

Family Planning – PLEASE USE REAR ENTRANCE.
Sign outside the Barnstable Health Centre

CORRUPTION

I have often noticed that a bribe . . . has that effect
– it changes a relation. The man who offers a bribe
gives away a little of his own importance; the
bribe once accepted, he becomes the inferior, like a
man who has paid for a woman.
Graham Greene

Don't take a nickel, just hand them your business
card.
Richard M. Daley (1902-1975), American politician

I am against government by crony.
Harold L. Ickes (1874-1952), American politician,
resignation speech

COWARDICE

I'm a hero with coward's legs.
Spike Milligan, British comedian and writer

If you can't stand the heat, get out of the kitchen.
Harry S. Truman (1884-1972)

CONSCIENCE

Conscience and cowardice are really the same
things. Conscience is the trade name of the firm.
Oscar Wilde, The Picture of Dorian Gray, 1891

Conscience: the still small voice that makes you
feel still smaller.
James A. Sanaker

Conscience is the inner voice that warns us that
someone may be looking.
H. L. Mencken, Sententiae, 1920

CREATIVE ARTS

Skill without imagination is craftsmanship and gives us many useful objects such as wickerwork picnic baskets. Imagination without skill gives us modern art.
Tom Stoppard

Modern art is what happens when painters stop looking at girls and persuade themselves that they have had a better idea.
John Ciardi (1916-1986), writer and critic

One sees a square lady with three breasts and a guitar up her crotch.
Noel Coward, speaking of modern art

I can truthfully say that the painter has observed the Ten Commandments. Because he hath not made to himself the likeness of anything in heaven above, or that which is on earth beneath, or that which is in the water under the earth.
Abraham Lincoln, giving his opinion of a painting

Señor Dali, born delirious,
Considers it folly to be serious.
Phyllis McGinley (1904-1982), 1960, of painter
Salvador Dali

M. Cezanne must be some kind of a lunatic, afflicted with delirium tremens while he is painting. In fact, it is one of the weird shapes thrown off by hashish, borrowed from a swarm of ridiculous dreams.
French critic of painter, Paul Cezanne (1839-1906)

You are first in the decadence of your art.
Charles Baudelaire, of Edouard Manet (1832-1883)

The only genius with an IQ of 60.
Gore Vidal, of Andy Warhol (1930-1980)

CRICKET

The days of women's cricket being seen as a knicker parade must be over.
Norma Izard, manager of England's World Cup winners, 1993

Cricket is not a twentieth century game and nearly all modern-minded people dislike it.
George Orwell, 1944

I do not play cricket, because it requires me to assume such indecent positions.
Oscar Wilde

My wife had an uncle who could never walk down the nave of his abbey without wondering whether it would take spin.
Lord Home, British politician and statesman

It's a funny kind of month, October. For the really keen cricket fan it's when you discover that your wife left you in May.
Denis Norden

I do love cricket – it's so very English.
Sarah Bernhardt (1844-1923), French actress, on seeing a game of football

Well, there's Neil Harvey standing at leg slip with his legs apart waiting for a tickle.
Brian Johnston, sports commentator, as the Australian batsman fielded at Headingley in 1961

CRIME

Crimes, like virtues, are their own rewards.
George Farquhar (1678-1707), Irish dramatist

Far more university graduates are becoming criminals every year than are becoming policemen.
Philip Goodhart, British Conservative politician

I'm too embarrassed to go to the police.
Norman Webster, garage mechanic plagued by a mystery caller who plays Des O'Connor records down his phone

I think crime pays. The hours are good, you travel a lot.
Woody Allen, *Take the Money and Run,* 1969

I am laughing to think what risks you take to try to find money in a desk by night where the legal owner can never find any by day.
Honore de Balzac (1799-1850), French novelist, said on waking to find a burglar in the room. (attrib.)

Thieves respect property; they merely wish the property to become their property that they may more perfectly respect it.
G. K. Chesterton, *The Man Who was Thursday,* 1908

I'm all for bringing back the birch. But only between consenting adults.
Gore Vidal

Crime, like virtue, has its degrees.
Jean Racine (1639-1699), French dramatist

I found it quite restful in the cell because there was no telephone and no one to badger me and I actually went to sleep in there. If I didn't have to be in the Commons soon, I could have happily stayed there all day.
Tony Banks, MP, after being released by police following a protest in which he was chained to railings in London

One of my mates has shoplifted a copy already. He told me he wanted to read it but he wasn't about to pay money for it.
Ronnie Biggs, Great Train Robber, on his book *Odd Man Out*

The tragic lesson of guilty men walking free in this country has not been lost on the criminal community.
Richard M. Nixon

Death is one of the worst things that can happen to a Cosa Nostra member, and many prefer to pay a fine.
Woody Allen, *A Look at Organized Crime, New Yorker*

CRITICISM

Criticism is above all a gift, an intuition, a matter of tact and flair, it cannot be taught or demonstrated – it is an art.
Henri Amiel

I have the worst ear for criticism: even when I have created a stage set I like, I always hear the woman in the back of the dress circle who says she doesn't like blue.
Cecil Beaton

Criticism – a big bite out of someone's back.
Elia Kazan

Criticism of the arts in London, taken by and large, ends in a display of suburban omniscience which sees no further than the next door garden.
Sir Thomas Beacham

If the critics were always right we should be in deep trouble.
Robert Morley

People ask you for criticism but they only want praise.
W. Somerset Maugham

Criticism may not be agreeable, but it is necessary. It fulfils the same function as pain in the body. It calls attention to an unhealthy state of things.
Sir Winston Churchill

It's only the best fruit the birds pick at.
Bette Davis

It is much easier to be critical than to be correct.
Benjamin Disraeli

I love criticism just so long as it's unqualified praise.
Noel Coward

Two cheers for Democracy; one because it admits variety and two because it permits criticism.
E. M. Forster, Two Cheers for Democracy

Honest criticism means nothing: what one wants is unrestrained passion, fire for fire.
Henry Miller, Sexus, 1949

In Australia there is no such thing as constructive criticism.
George Mikes, Boomerang – Australia Rediscovered, 1968

On criticism – Preoccupied with what concerns it particularly, its own field, literature, it will soon lose sight of what concerns us, painting.
Paul Gauguin

. . . and the **critics**

Listening to the critics is like letting Muhammad Ali decide which astronaut goes to the moon.
Robert Duvall, film star

A bad review is like baking a cake with all the best ingredients and having someone sit on it.
Danielle Steel, novelist

Critics – murderers!
Samuel Taylor Coleridge

Great critics, of whom there are piteously few, build a home for the truth.
Raymond Chandler

To an anonymous critic – Thou eunuch of language; thou pimp of gender, murderous accoucheur of infant learning, thou pickle-herring in the puppet show of nonsense.
Robert Burns

A critic is a man who knows the way but can't drive the car.
Kenneth Tynan

Time is the only critic without ambition.
John Steinbeck

Critics are like eunuchs in a harem: they know how it's done, they've seen it done every day, but they're unable to do it themselves.
Brendan Behan

New York critics – I hear when one of them watched *A Star is Born,* he talked back to the screen.
Barbra Streisand, film star

Critics! Appalled. I venture on the name,
Those cut-throat bandits in the paths of fame.
Robert Burns, *Third Epistle to Robert Graves*

Some critics are emotionally desiccated, personally about as attractive as a year-old peach in a single girl's refrigerator.
Mel Brooks

I doubt whether art needed Ruskin any more than a moving train needs one of its passengers to shove it.
Tom Stoppard, of John Ruskin, author and art critic

Shaw, you ought to be roasted alive: though even then, you would not be to my taste.
Sir James Barrie of George Bernard Shaw

CULTS

What's a cult? It just means not enough people to make a minority.
Robert Altman

My son has taken up meditation – at least it's better than sitting doing nothing.
Max Kauffmann

CYNICISM

A man who knows the price of everything and the value of nothing.
Oscar Wilde, *Lady Windermere's Fan,* 1892

A cynic is just a man who found out when he was about ten that there wasn't any Santa Claus, and he's still upset.
James Gould Cozzens (1903-1978), American author

DANCE

These sort of boobies think that people come to balls to do nothing but dance; whereas everyone knows that the real business of balls is either to look out for a wife, to look after a wife, or to look after somebody else's wife.
R. S. Surtees (1803-1864), English novelist

Dancing with abandon, turning a tango into a fertility rite.
Marshall Pugh, British journalist and author

Dancing is a wonderful training for girls; it's the first way you learn to guess what a man is going to do before he does it.
Christopher Morley

I just put my feet in the air and move them round.
Fred Astaire (1899-1987)

Teenagers and old people may know how to dance, but real people who go to real parties haven't the slightest. The only dances they even half remember how to do are the ones they learned twenty years ago. This is what the old Supremes tape is for: stiff and overweight versions of the Jerk, The Mashed Potato, the Pony, the Swim, and the Watusi. And after six drinks everyone will revert to the Twist.
P. J. O'Rourke

DEBAUCHERY

My main problem is reconciling my gross habits with my net income.
Errol Flynn (1909-1959)

His face was filled with broken commandments.
John Masefield (1878-1967) English poet and playwright

Not joy, but joylessness, is the mother of debauchery.
Friedrich Nietzsche

DEBT

If it isn't the sheriff, it's the finance company. I've got more attachments on me than a vacuum cleaner.
John Barrymore

In the midst of life we are in debt.
Ethel Watts Mumford (1878-1940), American novelist and humorous writer

Creditors have better memories than debtors.
Benjamin Franklin (1706-1790)

Never run into debt, not if you can find anything else to run into.
Josh Billings, The Complete Works of Josh Billings, 1919

Some people use one half of their ingenuity to get into debt, and the other half to avoid paying it.
George D. Prentice (1802-1870), American poet and journalist

Anyone who lives within his means suffers from lack of imagination.
Lionel Stander

Solvency is entirely a matter of temperament and not of income.
Logan Pearsall Smith (1865-1946), American-born British writer

DESIRE

I have to find a girl attractive or it's like trying to start a car without an ignition key.
Jonathan Aitken, British politician

Where they love they do not desire and where they desire they do not love.
Sigmund Freud (1865-1939) Austrian psychiatrist

I write to be sexually desirable.
Kenneth Tynan, writer, to his wife

Better murder an infant in its cradle than nurse an unacted desire.
William Blake (1757-1827)

DIET

I am at a time of life when a general overhaul – a complete service, so to speak – might well extend my roadworthiness for another decade.
Roy Hattersley, British Labour MP, announcing he is going on a diet

My secret is that when I'm sitting at a table, I must see the whole meal set out before me. That way my body knows I can't eat it all.
Luciano Pavarotti, opera singer, attributing his six stone weight loss to brain power

Pavarotti is more likely to be in love with a plateful of spaghetti.
Wife of opera singer Pavarotti, speaking of their relationship

Not for me the heresies of healthy eating favoured by Edwina Currie, or the hypochondriacal fears of cholesterol.
Lord Hailsham

If you have formed the habit of checking on every new diet that comes along, you will find that, mercifully, they all blur together, leaving you with only one definite piece of information – French fried potatoes are out.
Jean Kerr, *Please Don't Eat the Daisies,* 1957

Health food may be good for the conscience but Oreos taste a hell of a lot better.
Robert Redford, American actor

I've been on a constant diet for the last two decades. I've lost a total of 789 pounds. By all accounts, I should be hanging from a charm bracelet.
Erma Bombeck

A really busy person never knows how much he weighs.
Edgar Watson Howe, Country Town Sayings, 1911

My wife is on a diet. Coconuts and bananas. She hasn't lost any weight, but can she climb a tree!
Henny Youngman

I went on a diet, swore off drinking and heavy eating, and in fourteen days I lost two weeks.
Joe E. Lewis

Health should be the goal, not thinness.
Jane Fonda, US actress

It's a losing battle for me even to try to be skinny; I'd be fighting it every single day. Besides, I've got better things to do. It makes me angry when I see beautiful big women wasting their time dieting. They're told they can't have anything unless they're thin – everyone's brainwashed.
Dawn French, British actress and comedienne

Unnecessary dieting is because everything from television and fashion ads have made it seem wicked to cast a shadow. This wild, emaciated look appeals to some women, though not to many men who are seldom seen pinning up a *Vogue* illustration in a machine shop.
Peg Bracken, US writer and humorist, *The I Hate to Cook Book,* 1960

DINNER PARTIES

Don't talk about yourself; it will be done when you leave.
Addison Mizner (1872-1933), American architect and writer

A dinner lubricates business.
Lord Stowell (1745-1836), English lawyer

The best number for a dinner party is two – myself and a dam' good waiter.
Nubar Gulbenkian (1897-1972), oil millionaire

Take counsel in wine, but resolve afterwards in water.
Benjamin Franklin (1706-1790)

It isn't so much what's on the table that matters as what's on the chairs.
W. S. Gilbert (1836-1911), English librettist

In dinner talk it is perhaps allowable to fling any faggot rather than let the fire go out.
J. M. Barrie (1860-1937), British playwright

DISHONESTY

It is almost always worth while to be cheated; people's little frauds have an interest which more than repays what they cost us.
Logan Pearsall Smith, *Afterthoughts,* 1931

He's the only man I every knew who had rubber pockets so he could steal soup.
Wilson Mizner, of a Hollywood studio chief

DIVORCE

For a while I pondered whether to take a vacation or get a divorce. We decided that a trip to Bermuda is over in two weeks, but a divorce is something you always have.
Woody Allen

The happiest time of anyone's life is just after the first divorce.
John Kenneth Galbraith

You don't know a woman till you've met her in court.
Norman Mailer

Divorce is the sacrament of adultery.
French proverb

Getting divorced just because you don't love a man is almost as silly as getting married just because you do.
Zsa Zsa Gabor

Fission after fusion.
Rita Mae Brown

So many persons think divorce a panacea for every
ill, who find out, when they try it, that the remedy
is worse than the disease.
Dorothy Dix (1861-1951), American journalist

No one should dare take him out of prison
without my agreement. From jail, he should go
only to his grave.
The wife of Yehi Eliahu, who has been in jail in Israel
for 31 years for refusing to give her a divorce

I have no wish for a second husband. I had enough
of the first. I like to have my own way – to lie
down mistress, and get up master.
Susanna Moodie (1803-1885), Canadian writer and
poet, *Roughing It in the Bush,* 1852

DRINK

Work is the curse of the drinking class.
Oscar Wilde

A lot of guys wake up feeling like shit. I'd pass out
for a couple of days.
John Daly, golfer, on drinking

I think I'm on the verge of a serious headache.
Stuart Barnes, England stand-off, after victory over
Scotland

I think lager is a brown liquid for people who like
to look as though they're drinking beer but don't
like the taste.
Kenneth Clarke, Chancellor of the Exchequer

There are no licensing laws in the House of
Commons, so alcohol is freely available all day
and all night. This, no doubt, plays a large part in
lowering inhibitions, which are dropped along
with the trousers.
Teresa Gorman, MP

Even though a number of people have tried, no one has yet found a way to drink for a living.
Jean Kerr, US dramatist and humorist, *Poor Richard*

Actually, it only takes one drink to get me loaded. Trouble is, I can't remember if it's the thirteenth or fourteenth.
George Burns

By all means, let's breath-test pedestrians involved in road accidents – if they're still breathing.
The Bishop of Ely, 1967

A woman drove me to drink and I never even had the courtesy to thank her.
W. C. Fields, (attrib.)

I always wake up at the crack of ice.
Joe E. Lewis

My dad was the town drunk. A lot of times that's not so bad – but New York City?
Henny Youngman

No poems can please for long or live that are written by water-drinkers.
Horace (65-8BC), Roman poet and satirist

The reason I drink is because when I'm sober I think I'm Eddie Fisher.
Dean Martin, American actor

Brandy and water spoils two good things.
Charles Lamb

I prefer the bar to the gym any day. I like to drink and I like to brawl.
Sean Penn, American actor

Health is what my friends are always drinking to before they fall down.
Phyllis Diller

Most British statesmen have either drunk too much or womanised too much. I never fell into the second category.
Lord George Brown, Labour MP

The trouble with the world is that it's always one drink behind.
Humphrey Bogart (1899-1957)

My father considered that anyone who went to chapel and didn't drink alcohol was not to be tolerated. I grew up in that belief.
Richard Burton

Hell, I used to take two-week lunch hours!
Spencer Tracy (1900-1967)

I try not to drink too much because when I'm drunk, I bite.
Bette Midler

Lady Booze is a very cruel mistress.
John Hurt

Drinking removes warts and pimples. Not from me, but from those I look at.
Jackie Gleason (1916-87)

DRINKING

A fuddled woman is a shameful sight, a prey to anyone and serve her right.
Ovid (Publius Ovidius Naso) (43BC-AD17), Roman poet

If I picked up a drink I could kill myself. That's the knowledge I have. One is too many and a thousand isn't enough.
Eric Clapton, musician, on drinking

They who drink beer will think beer.
Washington Irving (1783-1859), American author

I had the happiest days of my life as a drinker. If I had my life again I'd make all the same mistakes . . . I would still sleep with as many women, and drink as much vodka. Any regrets would make me seem ungrateful.
Richard Harris

Bring in the bottled lightning, a clean tumbler, and a corkscrew.
Charles Dickens (1812-1870)

A man who exposes himself when he is intoxicated, has not the art of getting drunk.
Dr Samuel Johnson

A soldier must not get drunk more often than once a week. It would, of course, be better if he did not get drunk at all, but one should not expect the impossible.
Genghis Khan (1162-1227)

Better belly burst than good liquor be lost.
Jonathan Swift (1667-1745)

Drunkenness is temporary suicide.
Bertrand Russell

I distrust camels – and anyone else who can go for a week without a drink.
Joe E. Lewis

There are two things that will be believed of any man whatsoever, and one of them is that he has taken to drink.
Booth Tarkington (1869-1946), American author

Your average British man likes to go and have a pint in the pub and enjoy it, and it's an intelligent man who can go there and know his limits.
Graeme Souness, Scottish footballer

Water in moderation cannot hurt anybody.
Mark Twain

Maybe that's a commentary on our society, that people try to get away from everything by getting drunk.
Terry Wogan, Irish chat-show host

Claret is the liquor for boys; port for me; but he who aspires to be a hero must drink brandy.
Samuel Johnson, Life of Johnson, J. Boswell

It costs money to die of cirrhosis of the liver.
P. G. Wodehouse

Drink'll wrinkle your winkle.
The Sun

I first started drinking at the age of seven when I found a bottle of sherry that my mother had won in a raffle, drank it, threw up, was out cold for about a day and wasn't forgiven easily by my mum.
Simon Bates, radio presenter, *A Really Useful Guide to Alcohol*

Gin was mother's milk to her.
George Bernard Shaw, *Pygmalion,* 1912

Under the Cathedral-church at Hereford is the greatest Charnelhouse for bones, that ever I saw in England . . . Cunning ale wives put the Ashes of these bones in their Ale to make it intoxicating.
John Aubrey (1626-1697)

One more drink and I'll be under the host.
Dorothy Parker

As long as it looks like alcohol . . . just act tiddly and no one will notice!
Edwina Currie, MP

O God that men should put an enemy in their mouths to steal away their brains.
William Shakespeare

A man is never drunk if he can lay on the floor without holding on.
Joe E. Lewis

DRUGS

The worst drug of today is not smack or pot – it's refined sugar.
George Hamilton, American actor

Is marijuana addictive? Yes, in the sense that most of the really pleasant things in life are worth endlessly repeating.
Richard Neville, Australian journalist

I'll die young, but it's like kissing God.
Lenny Bruce (1923-1966)

Now he's gone and joined that stupid club.
Mother of rock star suicide victim, Kurt Cobain,
referring to the early death of other rock stars

I was a rhinestoned cowboy.
Glen Campbell, talking of drug addiction

Avoid all needle drugs – the only dope worth
shooting is Richard Nixon.
Abbie Hoffman, *Steal This Book,* 1971

Drugs have taught an entire generation of
American kids the metric system.
P. J. O'Rourke, *Modern Manners,* 1983

If you can stay in love for more than two years,
you're *on* something.
Fran Lebowitz

It's not enough to catch a stable lad with a
smoking syringe.
Roger Buffham, head of Jockey Club security, on the
difficulties of bringing convictions for doping

When I went to the South American championship in Columbia in 1977, from a squad of 30 players there were 20 on drugs.
Carlos Bilardo, former Argentina manager on Claudio Caniggia's suspension for cocaine use

Pot is like a gang of Mexican bandits in your brain. They wait for thoughts to come down the road, then tie them up and trash them.
Kevin Rooney, journalist

Drugs, I have stayed away from. It was exciting, dealing. It was stimulating. I've always lived on the edge. I've enjoyed that. And it was very challenging. But do I use drugs recreationally? No, no, no.
Roger Clinton, brother of USA President Bill Clinton

Happiness is like coke – something you get as a by-product in the process of making something else.
Aldous Huxley, Point Counter Point

Cocaine is God's way of saying you're making too much money.
Robin Williams

One man's poison is another man's drug.
Father Ronald Knox (1888-1957), British clergyman and writer

The only reason that cocaine is such a rage today is that people are too dumb and lazy to get themselves together to roll a joint.
Jack Nicholson

Thou hast the keys of Paradise, oh just, subtle, and mighty opium!
Thomas de Quincey (1785-1859), English author

They should have called me Little Cocaine, I was sniffing so much of the stuff! My nose got big enough to back a diesel truck in, unload it, and drive it right out again.
Little Richard

Every form of addiction is bad, no matter whether the narcotic be alcohol or morphine or idealism.
Carl Gustav Jung (1875-1961), Swiss psychoanalyst, *Memories, Dreams, Reflections*

Cocaine isn't habit-forming. I should know – I've been using it for years.
Tallulah Bankhead (1902-1968), American actress

Realism is just a crutch for people who can't cope with drugs.
Lily Tomlin

Now they're calling taking drugs an epidemic – that's 'cos white folks are doing it.
Richard Pryor, *Richard Pryor Here and Now*, 1984

. . . conversation degenerates in an exponential relationship to the amount of mood-altering substances one has recently ingested. Cocaine, marijuana and ethyl alcohol fall into this category. Sex, or a lack thereof, and Hershey bars are also mood-altering substances, which may explain why it is so difficult to speak to teenagers.
Tracy Young, British writer

If cannabis is legalised I'd like a packet of 20 to be called High.
Simon Bates, former Radio 1 DJ, and radio talk show presenter, calling for the legalisation of cannabis

I would like to have been druggy – the sort of boy that girls shake their heads over.
Hugh Grant, British actor

I mean, I'm not a bad person. I just made a mistake.
Patricia Cahill, British girl freed after being jailed for drug smuggling

Everyone here refers to the rugby pitch as the Field of Dreams.
Pupil at Dollar Academy, Scotland, after revelations that magic mushrooms grow naturally in the surrounding area

We postponed our wedding quite a while. I had
some things to clean up in my life. I was addicted
to drugs. I come from the drug culture of the
Sixties and early Seventies and back then, drugs
were fun. Then they became fun with problems.
And then for the last year, it was just problems.
Dennis Quaid, American actor

It is not opium which enables me to work, but its
absence; and to feel its absence it must from time
to time pass through me.
Antonin Artaud (1896-1948), French theatre producer
and actor

I was earning a fortune and it was terrific fun. But
the stress became too much. I went to parties and
smoked pot – it was the only way to relax.
Joanna Lumley, actress

I did drugs to keep going. But performing in itself
is a drug and taking cocaine is like being a
haemophiliac in a razor factory.
Robin Williams

Don't smoke, don't drink, don't eat much.
Have a sniff of this.
Victor Spinetti, comedian, recalling the first words that
actor Tony Curtis said on meeting him

EATING

The best number for a dinner party is two – myself
and a dam' good head waiter.
Nubar Gulbenkian (1897-1972), oil millionaire

Seeing is deceiving. It's eating that's believing.
James Thurber, Further Fables For Our Time, 1956

How to eat like a child: Chocolate-chip cookies:
half-sit, half-lie on the bed, propped up by a
pillow. Read a book. Place cookies next to you on
the sheet so that crumbs get in the bed. As you eat
the cookies, remove each chocolate chip and place
it on your stomach. When all the cookies are
consumed, eat the chips one by one, allowing two
per page.
Delia Ephron

EDUCATION

When a woman inclines to learning there is usually something wrong with her sex apparatus.
Friedrich Nietzsche

Education is what you must acquire without any interference from your schooling.
Mark Twain

Teaching has ruined more American novelists than drink.
Gore Vidal

He is either dead or teaching school.
Zenobius, 100BC

Public schools are the nurseries of all vice and immorality.
Henry Fielding

A lot of fellows nowadays have a B.A., M.A., or Ph.D. Unfortunately they don't have a J.O.B.
Fats Domino

To educate a man in mind and not in morale is to educate a menace to society.
Theodore Roosevelt

For those of you who have studied or are studying for many years for your degrees this must seem positively cheeky, and I apologise. But you need idiots like me who are prepared to own animals of various shapes, sizes and descriptions.
The Princess Royal, after accepting an honorary doctorate in veterinary medicine

When I was a young man in the House I decided that the best qualification for the politician was to enjoy Dostoevsky.
Baron Healey of Riddlesden, MP

All schools claim to be 'caring', but frankly some of them are like St. Trinian's on a bad day.
Baroness Blatch, education minister

Just because you swallowed a fucking dictionary when you were about 15 doesn't give you the right to pour a bucket of shit over the rest of us.
Paul Keating, Australian finance minister, responding to a critic of his schooling, 1989

EGOTISM

If egotism means a terrific interest in one's self, egotism is absolutely essential to efficient living.
Arnold Bennett

I jumped out of bed and started taking bows. I thought it [the quake] was the audience applauding.
George Burns, American actor, joking about his experience in the Los Angeles earthquake

Egotist: n. a person . . . more interested in himself than in me.
Ambrose Bierce, *The Devil's Dictionary,* 1911

Egotism – usually just a case of mistaken nonentity.
Barbara Stanwyck

Talk to a man about himself and he will listen for hours.
Benjamin Disraeli

Shirley MacLaine is 56 and this is her sixth volume of autobiography. Even giant egomaniacs usually stop short of dividing their lives up into decade sized chunks, but then to read Ms MacLaine is to encounter one of the most inflated airheads ever to break free of her moorings.
John Preston, British journalist

He moves like a parody between a majorette girl and Fred Astaire.
Truman Capote, of Mick Jagger

She only went to Venice because someone told her she could walk down the middle of the street.
Neil Kinnock, MP, of Margaret Thatcher, attending a conference in Venice

I am always a little more exaggerated and extrovert for the lights and the cameras and the people. I think, sometimes I am Jean Paul Gaultier the designer, sometimes I am Jean Paul Gaultier the television person and sometimes I am neither.
Jean Paul Gaultier

It's nice to be part of history, but people should get it right. I may not be perfect, but I'm bloody close.
John Lydon, formerly Johnny Rotten

I was wrong in believing there was a man capable of hiding what pleases his vanity.
Marie de La Fayette (1634-1693), French novelist, *The Princess of Cleves*

ENVY

Envy is capable of serving the valuable social function of making the rich moderate their habits for fear of arousing it.
Sir Keith Joseph, British Conservative politician

Moral indignation is in most cases two per cent moral, 48 per cent indignation and 50 per cent envy.
Vittorio De Sica (1901-1974), Italian film director

Not to be covetous is money in your purse; not to be eager to buy is income.
Cicero

People may go on talking for ever of the jealousies of pretty women; but for real genuine, hard-working envy, there is nothing like an ugly woman with a taste for admiration.
Emily Eden (1797-1869), British-born Indian novelist

Fools may our scorn, not envy raise,
For envy is a kind of praise.
John Gay (1685-1732), English poet and dramatist, *Fables*

The 'Green Eyed Monster' causes much woe, but the absence of this ugly serpent argues the presence of a corpse whose name is Eros.
Minna Antrim, US writer, *Naked Truth and Veiled Allusions*, 1902

His scorn of the great is repeated too often to be real; no man thinks much of that which he despises.
Dr Samuel Johnson (1709-1784)

Though jealousy be produced by love, as ashes are by fire, yet jealousy extinguishes love as ashes smother the flame.
Margaret of Navarre (1492-1549), French poet, writer, *The Fifth Day*

The dullard's envy of brilliant men is always assuaged by the suspicion that they will come to a bad end.
Sir Max Beerbohm (1872-1936), British writer and caricaturist, *Zuleika Dobson*

In a consumer society there are inevitably two kinds of slaves: the prisoners of addition and the prisoners of envy.
Ivan Illich, Austrian sociologist, *Tools for Conviviality*

EROTICISM

She has been described as the Maharanee of Malice, the Empress of Erotica, the Princess of Pulp, the Pasha of Porn. Despite having received the most spectacularly worst reviews ever written in India, she is the country's bestselling writer.
The Sunday Times Magazine, profile on Indian author Shobhan De

I am reading everything she is writing. In one book, I am counting seventy-three copulations. I am shocked only.
Really – her head is full of perversions.
Mr Satish Lal, who makes carbuncle grinders in Bangalore, on Shobhan De

Women have been complaining to us for years that there is nothing like this on the market. They have a right to look at erotic pictures of beautiful men. They want explicit articles about sex. After all, men have been open and free about their sexuality for a long time.
Isabel Koprowski, the former editor of *Forum,* on the launch of *For Women* magazine

EVIL

All men are evil and will declare themselves to be so when occasion is offered.
Sir Walter Raleigh (1552-1618)

When choosing between two evils, I always like to try the one I've never tried before.
Mae West (1892-1980)

Wickedness is a myth invented by good people to account for the curious attractiveness of others.
Oscar Wilde, 1894

There is no worse evil than a bad woman; and nothing has ever been produced better than a good one.
Euripides (480-406BC), Greek dramatist, *Melanippe*

Of two evils, choose the prettier.
Carolyn Wells (1870-1942), American writer

EVILS OF HOUSEWORK

Any woman who understands the problems of running a home will be nearer to understanding the problems of running a country.
Margaret Thatcher, 1979

Housekeeping ain't no joke.
Louisa May Alcott (1832-1888), US novelist, *Little Women*

I make no secret of the fact that I would rather lie on a sofa than sweep beneath it. But you have to be efficient if you're going to be lazy.
Shirley Conran, British designer and journalist, *Superwoman*, 1975

Cleaning your house while your kids are still growing
Is like shovelling the walk before it stops snowing.
Phyllis Diller, US writer and comedienne, *Phyllis Diller's Housekeeping Hints*, 1966

EXAMINATIONS

Yes, I could have been a judge but I never had the Latin for the judging. I just never had sufficient of it to get through the rigorous judging exams. They're noted for their rigour. People come staggering out saying, 'My God, what a rigorous exam'. And so I became a miner instead. A coal miner. I managed to get through the mining exams – they're not very rigorous. They only ask you one question; they say 'Who are you?' and I got seventy-five per cent on that.
Peter Cook, *Sitting on a Bench*, nightclub act, 1960s

Examinations are formidable even to the best prepared, for the greatest fool may ask more than the wisest man can answer.
C. C. Colton (1780-1832), English author and clergyman

I was thrown out of college for cheating on the metaphysics exam: I looked into the soul of another boy.
Woody Allen

EXCESS

I hate to advocate drugs, alcohol, violence, or insanity to anyone, but they've always worked for me.
Hunter S. Thompson

I have not been afraid of excess: excess on occasion is exhilarating. It prevents moderation from acquiring the deadening effect of a habit.
W. Somerset Maugham, *The Summing Up,* 1938

Moderation is a fatal thing. Nothing succeeds like excess.
Oscar Wilde, *A Woman of No Importance,* 1893

The road of excess leads to the palace of wisdom.
William Blake (1757-1827)

EXCUSES

. . . I am prevented from coming in consequence of a subsequent engagement. I think that would be a rather nice excuse: it would have all the surprise of candour.
Oscar Wilde, *The Picture of Dorian Gray,* 1891

. . . several excuses are always less convincing than one.
Aldous Huxley, *Point Counter Point,* 1928

Fish fuck in it.
W. C. Fields (1880-1946), US actor, giving his reason for not drinking water (attrib.)

E X E R C I S E

That's not exercise, it's flagellation.
Noel Coward (1899-1973), of squash

Exercise is bunk. If you are healthy you don't need it, if you are sick you shouldn't take it.
Henry Ford (1863-1947)

I love long walks, especially when they are taken by people who annoy me.
Fred Allen (1894-1957), American comic

I get my exercise acting as a pallbearer to my friends who exercise.
Chancey Depew (1834-1928), American Republican politician

Whenever I feel like exercise, I lie down until the feeling passes.
Robert M. Hutchins (1899-1977), American educator and writer

His favourite exercise is climbing tall people.
Phyllis Diller, of Mickey Rooney

I bought all those Jane Fonda videos. I love to sit and eat cookies and watch 'em.
Dolly Parton

I'm Jewish. I don't work out. If God had wanted us to bend over he'd put diamonds on the floor.
Joan Rivers

I have never taken any exercise, except for sleeping and resting, and I never intend to take any. Exercise is loathsome.
Mark Twain

Jogging is for people who aren't intelligent enough to watch Breakfast TV.
Victoria Wood, comedienne

The only reason I would take up jogging is so that I could hear heavy breathing again.
Erma Bombeck

The only exercise I get is when I take the studs out of one shirt and put them in another.
Ring Lardner

FAILURE

That poor man. He's completely unspoiled by failure.
Noel Coward, of a fellow playwright

We women adore failures. They lean on us.
Oscar Wilde, A Woman of No Importance, 1893

FAME

Fame is being asked to sign your autograph on the back of a cigarette packet.
Billy Connolly

You're always a little disappointing in person because you can't be the edited essence of yourself.
Mel Brooks

In the future everyone will be famous for fifteen minutes.
Andy Warhol

Fame is a powerful aphrodisiac.
Graham Greene, British novelist

FANATICISM

Fanaticism consists in redoubling your effort when you have forgotten your aim.
George Santayana (1863-1952), American philosopher and poet

Defined in psychological terms, a fanatic is a man who consciously overcompensates a secret doubt.
Aldous Huxley

A fanatic is one who can't change his mind and won't change the subject.
Sir Winston Churchill

Fanatics are men with strong tastes for drink trying hard to keep sober.
Elbert Hubbard

There are few catastrophes so great and irremediable as those that follow an excess of zeal.
H. Benson (1871-1914), British novelist

Without fanaticism we cannot accomplish anything.
Eva Peron (1919-1952)

FANTASY

Sex, or sexual fantasy, the Mills & Boon tendency as I call it, is what leads some largely female selection committees to choose good looking young men rather than outspoken middle-aged women.
Teresa Gorman, MP

Fantastically voluptuous sex-kitten goddess needs major licking from a rich well-hung man.
Dawn French, actress and comedienne, when asked how she would describe herself in a lonely hearts ad

Fantasy love is much better than reality love. Never doing it is exciting. The most exciting attractions are between two opposites that never meet.
Andy Warhol

In my sex fantasy, nobody ever loves me for my mind.
Nora Ephron, American writer

FASHION

No advert for a country that boasts Savile Row.
Wayne Robbins, journalist, of John Major

Princess Di wears more clothes in one day than
Gandhi wore in his whole life.
Joan Rivers

The talented, flamboyant drummer, whose
exhibitionist taste in fashion makes the typical
streetwalker's fare seem suitable for the corporate
boardroom.
Wayne Robbins, of Sheila E., 1987

Saint-Laurent has excellent taste. The more he
copies me, the better taste he displays.
Coco Chanel, of Yves Saint-Laurent, 1971

Boy George is all England needs – another queen
who can't dress.
Joan Rivers, of musician Boy George

He was clad in a black barrage balloon cleverly
painted to look like a dinner jacket.
Clive James, of actor Orson Welles

You don't have to signal a social conscience by
looking like a frump. Lace knickers won't hasten
the holocaust, you can ban the bomb in a feather
boa just as well as without, and a mild interest in
the length of hemlines doesn't necessarily
disqualify you from reading *Das Kapital* and
agreeing with every word.
Jill Tweedie (1936-1994), British journalist

Fashion is what one wears oneself. What is
unfashionable is what other people wear.
Oscar Wilde

By actual count, there are only six women in the
country who looked well in a jump-suit. Five of
them were terminal and the other was sired by a
Xerox machine.
Erma Bombeck, *If Life is a Bowl of Cherries,* 1978

To a woman, the consciousness of being well-dressed gives a sense of tranquility which religion fails to bestow.
Helen Olcott Bell (1830-1918), US writer, *Letters and Social Aims*, 1876

An after-dinner speech should be like a lady's dress – long enough to cover the subject and short enough to be interesting.
R. A. Butler (1902-1982), British Conservative politician

I cannot and will not cut my conscience to fit this year's fashions.
Lillian Hellman (1907-1984), American playwright

Fashion is made to become unfashionable.
Coco Chanel

Fashion is an imposition, a reign on freedom.
Golda Meir

Fashions, after all, are only induced epidemics.
G. B. Shaw

Fashion is a form of ugliness so intolerable that we have to alter it every six months.
Oscar Wilde

To call a fashion wearable is the kiss of death. No new fashion worth its salt is ever wearable.
Eugenia Shepherd, New York Herald Tribune, 1960

Fashion exists for women with no taste, etiquette for people with no breeding.
Queen Marie of Romania, 1938

Fashion is something barbarous, for it produces innovation without reason and imitation without benefit.
George Santayana

Our Norma went for a Crimplene full-frontal on the cover of the *Sunday Times Magazine.* Not only did she wear Crimplene, but it was brown Crimplene.
Time Out, of Norma Major, wife of the Prime Minister, 1992

FAUX PAS

Be careful.
Hartley Booth, MP, when asked what advice he had for
MPs who attract pretty women, after revelations of his
infidelity . . . He later added . . . 'I already regret making
that comment. My advice should have been that it's worse
than that. Just don't do it.'

They are absolutely on top of their brief.
John Major, speaking of his ministers

Mancini seems to have yards under his shorts.
Ray Wilkins, commentator

How wide do I have to open my legs?
Jeni Barnet, television presenter to waltz instructor

It was so romantic. He just took it out and put it
on the table in Soho.
Kathryn Holloway, presenter of *TV AM,* showing off
her engagement ring

I did it for six hours non-stop and afterwards I
couldn't keep by knees together for a fortnight.
Trish Williams, TV weather presenter, talking about
horse riding

BUENOS AIRES, April 1 (Reuter): Maradona,
downcast at his failure to resurrect his soccer
career, has said he was consulting his psychologist
over whether to give up the game for food.
The Times of India

If you're a groovy f***er, watch the Tube.
Jools Holland, TV presenter on live trailer for *The Tube,*
1986. The show was axed the following month

I would like to f*** you.
Serge Gainsbourg, propositioning Whitney Houston on
prime-time French television. . . the show host attempting
to cover Serge's slip, translated the line for French viewers
as: 'He means he wants to give her flowers. Quoi?'

We're not in control of this situation, because
Mother Nature is having its way with us as
periodically happens.
President Clinton, speaking about the US floods, 1993

You don't understand. I have to be on top.
Shirley MacLaine, American actress, reply to local
environmentalists protesting about her plans to build a
retreat on Atalaya Mountain – sacred to some local people

FEMININE WILES

I was characterised as a flame haired temptress, so
poor Norman Lamont, how could he possibly help
himself?
Ginny Dougary, The Times feature writer. When she
profiled Norman Lamont, her feature prompted howls of
outrage from male columnists, who accused her and other
women interviewers of using feminine wiles to coax
indiscretions from their subjects

What other women had to say on the subject:

The danger with women is that they think you're a
sister or a friend. I don't think there's any need to
act the bimbo to interview men. Listening with
rapt attention is far more seductive than a mile of
cleavage.
Lynn Barber, interviewer and columnist for *The Sunday
Times*

You can always pretend to be stupider than you
are. Men assume, oh the sweet little thing, she
won't understand. When I was on the Serbian
front line, half the time they didn't realise I was
asking hard questions.
Ann Leslie, writer for *The Daily Mail*

I don't think gender really is a factor in
interviewing. I can't tell, as I find interviewing
politicians the most deadly job in the world, as it's
their job not to say anything really interesting.
Barbara Amiel, columnist and interviewer for *The
Sunday Times*

Isn't every interview a seduction? You're seducing the subject into liking you enough to tell you things they never dreamed they were going to tell you. If Norman Lamont was stupid enough to fall for that, then more fool he.

If you're the best writer in the world but you look like the back end of a wart hog, you're going to have to prove yourself. If you look like Selina Scott, you have a lot more entrées and a better starting point.

Nina Myskow, columnist for *The Sun*

Like the way you look and the tone of your voice, gender does play some part in interviewing, but not in the crude way suggested by David Mellor. This image of the seductive creature who draws men out is unfounded. Of course people flirt, but most people flirt in a similar way and it's not very revealing.

Zoe Heller, feature writer for the *Independent on Sunday*

A Tory MP told me he believes a number of newspapers have junior women reporters whom they use to attract the men and bring back the gossip which they then write up. I find it rather embarrassing sometimes being kissed in the members' lobby. I know many politicians very well, as friends, but I find that embarrassing. They sometimes trust and confide in me in a way they wouldn't a man.

Julia Langdon, political writer

I find the reaction to Ginny Dougary's article really offensive. Nobody accused Dominic Lawson of batting his eyelids at Nicholas Ridley. Any politician who takes a pose during the interview and then cynically says what he really thinks over lunch should know what to expect. Men often think you're a silly girlie. I hate it when they see me taking shorthand during an interview and they say: 'Take this down!', as if they're dictating the interview.

Jan Moir, writer for *The Guardian*

I recently interviewed Steven Berkoff and since then, a story has been going round that I slept with him. This is completely untrue. I think he didn't like the interview.
Chrissie Iley, feature writer for *The Sunday Times*

When I was showbiz editor on *Today,* I would always send out reporters of the opposite sex to the interviewees. And personally I much prefer interviewing women. You get pretty young things from *The Sun* going out to interview hardened male actors who normally wouldn't give the paper the time of day. But as soon as they see this pretty blonde thing there's a chemistry which makes them talk. If an actor forgets they're in the room with a journalist, they'll drop their guard. That's the art of interviewing.
Lester Middlehurst, TV editor, *The Daily Mail*

Flirtation comes into it absolutely. I always make an effort to dress up to the level of the person I'm interviewing and I *love* interviewing women. It always tells me something about a woman's star qualities if I'm sexually attracted to her. If I'm not, then there's something wrong.
Baz Bamigboye, showbiz columnist, *The Daily Mail*

FETISHISM

Pumping is the devil's pastime, and we must all say no to Satan. Inflate your tyres by all means, but then hide your bicycle pump where it cannot tempt you.
The Japan Times, 1993, referring to the craze of pumping – sticking a bicycle nozzle up the rectum

Buttock fetishism is comparatively rare in our culture . . . Girls are often self-conscious about their behinds, draping themselves in long capes and tunics, but it is more often because they are too abundant in that region than otherwise.
Germaine Greer

Business was never better. It brought all the kinky
ones out of the closet.
Lindi St Clair, prostitute, founder of the Corrective
Party, 1988, following the exposure of a dungeon and
fetish chambers at her brothel

FLATTERY

Flattery is like a cigarette – it's all right so long as
you don't inhale.
Adlai Stevenson (1900-1965), American politician and
lawyer

The only man who wasn't spoiled by being
lionised was Daniel.
Sir H. Beerbohm Tree

What really flatters a man is that you think him
worth flattering.
George Bernard Shaw, John Bull's Other Island, 1904

Is there no beginning to your talents?
Clive Anderson, interviewing Jeffrey Archer,
Independent on Sunday, 1991

I'll tell you what I don't like about Christmas
office parties – looking for a new job afterwards.
Phyllis Diller

Imitation is the sincerest form of flattery.
Charles Caleb Colton (1780-1832), British clergyman
and writer

I can live for two months on a good compliment.
Mark Twain

Every woman is infallibly to be gained by every
sort of flattery, and every man by one sort or
other.
Earl of Chesterfield (1694-1773), English statesman

I have come to the conclusion that it is more
flattering to be a 'man's woman' than a 'woman's
woman': a man's woman has to be unselfish and
agreeable at any rate in conversation – with a
mind broader than her shop, as men have the
supreme merit of not always wanting to talk shop.
Freya Stark, British traveller and writer

Madam, before you flatter a man so grossly to his face, you should consider whether or not your flattery is worth his having.
Dr Samuel Johnson

Baloney is flattery so thick it cannot be true; blarney is flattery so thin we like it.
Bishop Fulton J. Sheen (1895-1979), American clergyman and author

It is the usual frailty of our sex to be fond of flattery. I blame this in other women, and should not wish to be chargeable with it myself.
Marguerite of Valois (1553-1615), French Queen and diarist

Just praise is only a debt, but flattery is a present.
Dr Samuel Johnson

FLIRTATION

Flirtation, attention without intention.
Max O'Rell (1848-1903), French journalist, lecturer and critic

No matter how happily a woman may be married, it always pleases her to discover that there is a nice man who wishes that she were not.
H. L. Mencken (1880-1956), American journalist and linguist

George Moore unexpectedly pinched my behind. I felt rather honoured that my behind should have drawn the attention of the great master of English prose.
Ilka Chase, American actress and writer

When she raises her eyelids, it's as if she were taking off all her clothes
Colette (1873-1954)

What attracts us in a woman rarely binds us to her.
J. Churton Collins (1848-1908), British author and critic

Men do make passes at girls who wear glasses –
but it all depends on their frames.
Optician, 1964

In order to avoid being called a flirt, she always
yielded easily.
Charles Talleyrand (1754-1838), French politician

Girls like to be played with and rumpled a little
too, sometimes . . .
Oliver Goldsmith (1728-1774), Irish playwright,
novelist and poet

FOOD

The national dish of America is menus.
Robert Robinson, British writer and broadcaster

To Gazza, ice cream is more important than his
credit cards.
Dino Zoff, manager of Lazio, who ordered Paul
Gascoigne to lose weight, 1993

That was nearly the most expensive lunch I ever
ate.
Liz Taylor, American film star, when she mislaid her
famous Krup diamond ring at a charity dinner – it was
later found

Is she fat? Her favourite food is seconds.
Joan Rivers, of Elizabeth Taylor

Is that an offer?
Edwina Currie, when asked if fruit ever played a part in
her love life, during an interview about her steamy novel *A
Parliamentary Affair*

Artichokes heat the genitals.
French saying

My bowels shall sound like an harp.
Isaiah, on eating beans, *The Bible*

I wouldn't eat 'Shredded Wheat'. I don't like
sawdust with milk all over it.
Ian Botham, cricketer

A delicatessen is a shop selling the worst parts of animals more expensively than the nice parts.
Mike Barfield, British writer and journalist

Part of the secret of success in life is to eat what you like and let the food fight it out inside.
Mark Twain

The right diet directs sexual energy into the parts that matter.
Barbara Cartland, British author

Everything you see, I owe to spaghetti
Sophia Loren, film star

Love, like a chicken salad or restaurant hash, must be taken with blind faith or it loses its flavour.
Helen Rowland, American writer

FOOLISHNESS

To be intimate with a foolish friend is like going to bed with a razor.
Benjamin Franklin (1706-1790), American scientist and philosopher, *Poor Richard's Almanack*, 1743

Nobody ever did anything very foolish except from some strong-principle.
Viscount William Lamb Melbourne (1779-1848), British statesman

If you are foolish enough to be contented, don't show it, but grumble with the rest.
Jerome K. Jerome (1859-1927), British dramatist

Mix a little foolishness with your serious plans: it's lovely to be silly at the right moment.
Horace (65-8 BC), Roman poet

Before God we are all equally wise – equally foolish.
Albert Einstein (1879-1955), German-born mathematical physicist

I'm not denying the women are foolish: God Almighty made 'em to match the men.
George Eliot (Mary Ann Evans) (1819-80), English novelist

I have great confidence in fools: self-confidence my friends will call it.
Edgar Allan Poe (1809-49), American writer

A fool and his words are soon parted: a man of genius and his money.
William Shenstone (1714-63), English gardener and poet

No woman of spirit thinks a man hath any respect for her 'till he hath plaid the fool in her service.
Sir Richard Steele (1672-1729), English essayist, *The Lowever*, 1714

FOOTBALL

Once we had a players' karaoke party. Gazza took off his clothes and sang Rod Stewart's 'Do you Think I'm Sexy?' There is no one like him. I wish we had someone like him. We Norwegians are boring.
Erik Thorstvedt, Tottenham and Norway goalkeeper, on Paul Gascoigne's socialising

Hump it, bump it, whack it might be one possible recipe for a good sex life, but it won't win us the World Cup.
Ken Bates, Chelsea chairman

I was playing football. This bloke opposite was giving me a really hard time so I left early, got the knife and was going to chop him. That's my problem . . . I don't argue.
A jailed Sunday footballer of Brixton, south London, on why he quit a game at half-time only to return with a handgun, ammunition and a machete

I'm as baffled as Adam on Mother's Day.
Xabier Azkargorta, Bolivian national football coach on the unavailability of players for his World Cup preparations

Some people think football is a matter of life and death . . . I can assure you it is much more serious than that.
Bill Shankly, 1973

Football is all very well as a game for rough girls, but it is hardly suitable for delicate boys.
Oscar Wilde (attrib.)

The centre forward said, 'It was an open goal – but I put it straight over the crossbar! I could kick myself!' And the manager said, 'I wouldn't bother, you'd probably miss!'
David Frost

FOUL PLAY

He could not see a belt without hitting below it.
Margot Asquith, wife of Prime Minister Herbert Asquith (1864-1945), of Lloyd George

Quit fouling like a wimp. If you're gonna foul, knock the crap outta him.
Norm Stewart, Missouri Tigers' basketball coach, to 6ft 9in Dan Bingenheimer

GAMBLING

The sure way of getting nothing for something.
Wilson Mizner (1876-1933), American dramatist and wit

There are two times in a man's life when he should not speculate: when he can't afford it, and when he can.
Mark Twain

The only man who makes money following the races is one who does it with a broom and shovel.
Elbert Hubbard (1865-1915), American author

It is the child of avarice, the brother of iniquity, and the father of mischief.
George Washington (1732-1799)

No wife can endure a gambling husband unless he is a steady winner.
Lord Dewar (1864-1930), British writer and politician

Gambling promises the poor what property performs for the rich – something for nothing.
George Bernard Shaw

Poker exemplifies the worst aspects of capitalism that have made our country so great.
Walter Matthau, American actor

GLUTTONY

Gluttony is emotional escape, a sign something is eating us.
Peter De Vries, US novelist, *Comfort me with Apples*

I look big because I am big. That's what makes me what I am. If I drop dead, that's how it's meant to be.
William Conrad, American television star, before his death. Doctors had warned him that his constant overeating was killing him.

Gluttony is not a secret vice.
Orson Welles, American actor

GOLF

Give me my golf clubs, fresh air and a beautiful partner, and you can keep my golf clubs and fresh air.
Jack Benny

Eric: My wife says if I don't give up golf, she'll leave me.
Ernie: That's terrible.
Eric: I know – I'm really going to miss her.
Eric Morecambe and Ernie Wise, *The Morecambe and Wise Joke Book,* 1979

I hope she [Gill] can do the thing right. Don't even ask about missing the Masters. I'm confident my wife can produce on time, even if I have to take her for a rough ride in the Porsche.
Nick Faldo, golfer, hoping childbirth would not affect his participation in the US Masters, 1993

The Coarse Golfer: one who has to shout 'Fore' when he putts.
Michael Green, *The Art of Coarse Golf,* 1967

Golf is a good walk spoiled.
Mark Twain

A day spent in a round of strenuous idleness.
William Wordsworth (1770-1850)

Golf is a game whose aim is to hit a very small ball into an even smaller hole, with weapons singularly ill-designed for the purpose.
Sir Winston Churchill (1874-1965)

The uglier a man's legs are, the better he plays golf. It's almost a law.
H. G. Wells, *Bealby,* 1915

I regard golf as an expensive way of playing marbles.
G. K. Chesterton (1874-1936), English critic, novelist and poet

Golf is an ineffectual attempt to direct an uncontrollable sphere into an inaccessible hole with instruments ill-adapted to the purpose.
Sir Winston Churchill

I'd rather watch a cabbage grow, than a man worrying his guts over a two-foot putt.
Michael Parkinson, TV presenter and writer. Parkinson was a former president of the Anti-Golf League

G O S S I P

A recent survey of 43 scientifically selected Famous People reveals that 20.9 per cent of all Famous People would rather pull out their own teeth than read another Random Note about Mick Jagger.
Rolling Stone, *Random Notes*

She always tells stories in the present vindictive.
Tom Pearce, British writer, 1957

The things most people want to know about are usually none of their business.
George Bernard Shaw

If only a quarter of the things written about me were true, I'd be completely pickled by now and would have sired half the children in the world.
Ian Botham, England cricketer

I don't at all like knowing what people say of me behind my back. It makes one far too conceited.
Oscar Wilde, An Ideal Husband, 1895

Gossip: sociologists on a mean and petty scale.
Woodrow Wilson (1856-1924)

Gossip is the opiate of the oppressed.
Erica Jong, Fear of Flying

Gossip is vice enjoyed vicariously.
Elbert Hubbard (1856-1915), American author

She poured a little social sewage into his ears.
George Meredith (1828-1909), English author

Show me someone who never gossips, and I'll show you someone who isn't interested in people.
Barbara Walters, American television personality

None are so fond of secrets as those who do not mean to keep them.
C. C. Colton (1780-1832), English author

Gossip is the art of saying nothing in a way that leaves practically nothing unsaid.
Walter Winchell (1897-1972), American columnist

The gossip of two women will destroy two houses.
Arabic proverb

GREED

Avarice is generally the last passion of those lives of which the first part has been squandered in pleasure, and the second devoted to ambition.
Dr Samuel Johnson

Avarice, the spur of Industry.
David Hume

Callous greed grows pious very fast.
Lillian Hellman

GRUDGES

To have a grievance is to have a purpose in life.
Eric Hoffer (1902-1983), American philosopher

GUILT

Guilt has very quick ears to an accusation.
Henry Fielding (1707-1754)

Let other pens dwell on guilt and misery.
Jane Austen (1775-1817), British novelist, *Mansfield Park*

And there isn't any way that one can get rid of the guilt of having a nice body by saying that one can serve society with it, because that would end up with oneself as what?
Margaret Drabble, British writer, *A Summer Bird Cage*

True guilt is guilt at the obligation one owes to oneself to be oneself.
R. D. Laing, British psychiatrist

HATRED

I never hate a man enough to give him his diamonds back.
Zsa Zsa Gabor

Always remember others may hate you, but those who hate you don't win unless you hate them. And then you destroy yourself.
Richard Nixon

No one delights more in vengeance than a woman.
Juvenal, Roman satirist, *Satires, c.*100AD

Heaven has no rage like love to hatred turned,
Nor hell a fury like a woman scorned.
William Congreve (1670-1729), British Restoration dramatist, *The Mourning Bride,* 1697

HOLLYWOOD

If Clinton had the choice of meeting Maggie
Thatcher to discuss world affairs or Barbra
Streisand, there is no doubt which one he would
choose. It would be Streisand every time. He's
fixated on Hollywood and its celebrities.
Tony Burton, New York columnist, 1993

I work at Paramount all day and Fox at night.
Mae West

Hollywood's a place where they'll pay you a
thousand dollars for a kiss, and fifty cents for your
soul.
Marilyn Monroe (1926-1962)

Hollywood is the only place in the world where an
amicable divorce means each one gets fifty per cent
of the publicity.
Lauren Bacall

Strip away the phoney tinsel of Hollywood and
you find the real tinsel underneath.
Oscar Levant (1906-1972), American pianist and
composer

To survive there, you need the ambition of a Latin-
American revolutionary, the ego of a grand opera
tenor, and the physical stamina of a cow pony.
Billie Burke (1885-1970), American actress

I look upon going to Hollywood as a mission
behind enemy lines. You parachute in, set up the
explosion, then fly out before it goes off.
Robert Redford

If you write about Hollywood, you can only write
farce. It's so way over the top, you can't believe it.
It's *Sunset Boulevard,* it really is. And it's cut-
throat at the same time.
Dirk Bogarde

If you stay in Beverley Hills too long, you become
a Mercedes.
Dustin Hoffman

In Hollywood, if you can't sing or dance, you wind up as an after-dinner speaker.
Ronald Reagan

When I'm 60, Hollywood will forgive me. I don't know for what, but they'll forgive me.
Steven Spielberg

Hollywood died on me as soon as I got there.
Orson Welles (1915-1985)

Hollywood is geared to cheat you left, right and bloody centre.
John Hurt

Growing up female in America. What a liability! You grew up with your ears full of cosmetic ads, love songs, advice columns, whorescopes. Hollywood gossip, and moral dilemmas on the level of TV soap operas. What litanies the advertisers of the good life chanted at you! What curious catechisms!
Erica Jong, Fear of Flying

Working for Warner Brothers is like fucking a porcupine. It's a hundred pricks against one.
Wilson Mizner (1876-1933), American dramatist and wit

I want a movie that starts with an earthquake and works up to a climax.
Samuel Goldwyn

You can fool all the people all the time if the advertising is right and the budget is big enough.
Joseph E. Levine, businessman

An associate producer is the only guy in Hollywood who will associate with the producer.
Fred Allen (1894-1957), American comic

You can seduce a man's wife there, attack his daughter and wipe your hands on his canary, but if you don't like his movie, you're dead.
Joseph von Sternberg (1894-1969), American director

Too caustic? To hell with the cost, we'll make the picture anyway.
Samuel Goldwyn (1882-1974)

The way things are going, I'd be more interested in seeing Cleopatra play the life of Elizabeth Taylor.
Earl Wilson, American author

You're not a star until they can spell your name in Karachi.
Humphrey Bogart (1899-1957)

God makes stars. I just produce them.
Samuel Goldwyn

One thing about being successful is that I stopped being afraid of dying. Once you're a star you're dead already. You're embalmed.
Dustin Hoffman

If my books had been any worse I should not have been invited to Hollywood, and if they had been any better, I should not have come.
Raymond Chandler

A movie without sex would be like a candy bar without nuts.
Earl Wilson, American columnist

It's Tom and Jerry. I love it and not just because of the money. I get to wear incredible disguises and be a character actor.
George Peppard (1929-1994), actor speaking of his role as Colonel Hannibal Smith in *The A-Team*, 1994

In Europe, an actor is an artist. In Hollywood, if he isn't working, he's a bum.
Anthony Quinn, actor

It's a big publicity contest. Oh, voting is legitimate, but there's the sentimentality. One year when I was a candidate, when Elizabeth Taylor got a hole in her throat, I cancelled my plane.
Shirley MacLaine, of the Oscar Awards

Filming with Streisand is an experience which may have cured me of movies.
Kris Kristofferson, American actor, 1981

She's common, she can't act – yet she's the hottest female property around these days. If that doesn't tell you something about the state of our industry today, what does?
Stewart Grainger, actor, of Joan Collins, 1984

How much talent, initiative, genius and creative ability have been destroyed by the film industry in its ruthlessly efficient sausage machine?
Ingmar Bergman, Swedish film and theatre director

Given the choice, of course, I would never go to bed. I'd drive right out to Hollywood five nights a week and party till dawn if I could. But, practically speaking, it's just not possible.
David Lee Roth, rock musician, admitting that at the end of the day he is so tired, that he goes to bed at 11 p.m., 1994

I'm a product of Hollywood; Fantasy is not unnatural to me, it's my reality.
Carrie Fisher, American film actress

HOMOSEXUALITY

Homosexual genital acts, even between mature, consenting adults, are objectively wrong.
Cardinal Hume, speaking for the Roman Catholic Church, 1994

In real life, I'm just a big plain Jane.
Andy Bell, pop singer, Erasure

The way things are going, it's more of a problem if MPs are heterosexual. They should be reversing the question and asking 'You're not a heterosexual are you?'
Matthew Parris, Times Columnist and former gay Tory MP, on reports that Conservative Central Office is pressuring suspected homosexual MPs to get married, 1994

My lesbianism is an act of Christian charity. All those women out there are praying for a man, and I'm giving them my share.
Rita Mae Brown, 1978

I became one of the stately homos of England.
Quentin Crisp, *The Naked Civil Servant,* 1968

It was out of the closet and into the streets for the nation's homosexuals in the seventies. This didn't do much for the streets, but on the other hand your average closet was improved immeasurably.
Rick Meyerowitz and John Weidman, National Lampoon, 1980

Hot, young and safe.
Poster on New York underground trains, showing homosexuals and lesbians holding condoms and other sexual devices

People who have a low self-esteem . . . have a tendency to cling to their own sex because it is less frightening.
Clare Thompson (1893-1958), US physician and writer

Does she want this House to legalise the buggery of adolescent males?
Tony Marlow, MP, to Edwina Currie, MP, during a debate on the lowering of the age of consent

This sort of thing may be tolerated by the French – but we are British, thank God.
Viscount Montgomery (1887-1976)

In America, of course, they're all homosexual.
Barbara Cartland

Just as if you eat food that doesn't nourish you, you eat more food. So people who indulge in unsatisfactory sex are often extraordinarily promiscuous.
Quentin Crisp

There is probably no sensitive heterosexual alive who is not preoccupied with his latent homosexuality.
Norman Mailer

When I see pictures of myself on stage dressed up in bizarre outfits and women's clothes, I think to myself – my God, I look like a big bloody lorry driver in drag.
Andy Bell, pop singer

Postumus, are you *really*
Taking a wife? . . .
Isn't it better to sleep with a pretty boy?
Boys don't quarrel all night, or nag you for little presents
While they're on the job, or complain that you don't come
Up to their expectations, or demand more gasping passion
Juvenal (60-130AD), Roman satirist, *Satires*

I never said I was 90 per cent gay. It's a ludicrous idea. As if I was counting up my chromosomes. And, without being too existentialist about it, one reinvents oneself every morning.
Stephen Fry, writer and actor

This is a celebration of individual freedom, not of homosexuality. No government has the right to tell its citizens when or whom to love. The only queer people are those who don't love anybody.
Rita Mae Brown, American feminist writer, of the Gay Olympics, 1982

I started to get letters from gay men saying they were delighted I'd come out of the closet. I haven't been in there!
Pete Townsend, British rock star, explaining one of the problems which arose when he released his song *Rough Boys*

I'd rather be black than gay because when you're black you don't have to tell your mother.
Charles Pierce, American female impersonator

This is a very sad day for democracy. MPs have decided that gay people should remain second class citizens.
Peter Tatchell, of pressure group Outrage, on hearing that MPs refused to lower the legal age for homosexual sex to 16, 1994

Cardinal Hume is saying it's all right to be homosexual as long as you are celibate. It's like saying to a black person that it's okay to be black as long as they cover up their black skin.
Tim Hopkins, of Outrage, after Cardinal Hume said that homosexual acts are morally wrong, 1993

He's just an old soddin' queen mincing around like some sickening Danny La Rue.
Ian McCulloch, of singer Boy George, 1985

Refusal to make herself the object is not always what turns women to homosexuality; most lesbians, on the contrary, seek to cultivate the treasures of their femininity.
Simone de Beauvoir (1908-1986), French writer and feminist

I have no doubt that lesbianism makes a woman virile and open to any sexual stimulation, and that she is more often than not, a more adequate and lively partner in bed than a 'normal' woman.
Charlotte Wolff, German-born British psychiatrist and writer, *Love Between Women,* 1971

The lesbian business was blown out of all proportion. I simply don't believe it.
Lady Flavia Leng, daughter of British writer, Daphne du Maurier, referring to revelations in a recently published biography of her mother, 1994

You're neither unnatural, nor abominable, nor mad; you're as much a part of what people call nature as anyone else; only you're unexplained as yet – you've not got your niche in creation.
Radclyffe Hall (1886-1943), British writer and poet, *The Well of Loneliness,* 1928

Lesbian is a label invented by man to throw at any woman who dares to be his equal, who dares to challenge his prerogatives . . . who dares to assert the primacy of her own needs.
Radicalesbians, *The Woman-Identified Woman,* 1970s

Once you know what women are like, men get kind of boring. I'm not trying to put them down; I mean I like them sometimes as people, but sexually they're dull.
Rita Mae Brown, American novelist

Don't say we are here because we get sexual gratification from seeing these women playing.
Lesbian attending the Pilkington Glass Ladies Tennis Championship, 1992, in which Martina Navratilova was playing

Gays grow up watching heterosexual movies –
Now Voyager – and deciding whether they're Bette
Davis or Paul Henreid.
Harvey Fierstein, writer-star of *Torch Song Trilogy*

I can tell that Christopher Reeve is not a
homosexual. When we kissed in *Deathtrap,* he
didn't close his eyes.
Michael Caine

HUNTING

If God didn't want man to hunt, he wouldn't have
given us plaid shirts.
Johnny Carson

No sportsman wants to kill the fox or the
pheasant as I want to kill him when I see him
doing it.
George Bernard Shaw

The English country gentleman galloping after a
fox – the unspeakable in full pursuit of the
uneatable.
Oscar Wilde, *A Woman of No Importance,* 1893

I only kill in self-defense. What would you do if a
rabbit pulled a knife on you?
Johnny Carson

When a man wants to murder a tiger he calls it
sport; when a tiger wants to murder him he calls it
ferocity.
George Bernard Shaw

HUSBANDS

A small band of men armed only with wallets,
besieged by a horde of wives and children.
National Lampoon, 1979

Husbands think we should know where everything is – like the uterus is the tracking device. He asks me, 'Roseanne, do we have any cheetos left?' Like he can't go over to that sofa cushion and lift it himself.
Roseanne Barr, American actress and comedienne

How would you like to be married to a man who says, 'I'm just going out to buy a newspaper, I'll be back in five minutes,' and doesn't come back for five weeks?
Elizabeth Rees-Williams, first wife of actor Richard Harris

An archaeologist is the best husband any woman can have; the older she gets, the more interested he is in her.
Agatha Christie

I do, and I also wash and iron them.
Dennis Thatcher replying to the question 'Who wears the pants in your house?', 1981

My husband had always hated me writing. What husbands and children really want is for you to have a proper job, like a dinner-lady.
Fay Weldon, writer

A husband is what is left of the lover after the nerve has been extracted.
Helen Rowland (1875-1950), American journalist

If there were no husbands, who would look after our mistresses?
George Moore, (1852-1933), Irish author

. . . a moody, broody Oriental. He was twenty years older than me, but it might as well have been a hundred. He was really three hundred years behind me.
Zsa Zsa Gabor, of her first husband, Burham Beige

Husbands are chiefly good lovers when they are betraying their wives.
Marilyn Monroe (1926-1962)

I don't sit around thinking that I'd like to have another husband; only another man would make me think that way.
Lauren Bacall, American actress

My idea of a superwoman is someone who scrubs her own floors.
Bette Midler, American singer and actress

You mean apart from my own?
Zsa Zsa Gabor, her reply when asked how many husbands she'd had.

Our courtship consisted of me waiting in the lobby, then meeting him, then being taken for a quick meal, then sitting in the committee room for a wee while. I had no illusions.
Sheila Taylor, wife of Sir Teddy, MP.

What about romance? When he comes home at the weekend, he's too bloody exhausted! We save that sort of thing up for the summer holidays. I mean it.
Eve Burt, wife of Alistair Burt, MP

No way. When the children were young I'd push a smelly nappy into his hands when he came through the door.
Alison Hayes, wife of Jerry Hayes, MP, when asked, 'When he [Jerry's] home, do you slip into a silk dressing gown?'

If you mean, do I put on a corset and suspenders and cook Julian asparagus on toast – then no I don't.
Katherine Brazier, wife of Julian Brazier, MP, when asked, 'What happens when your husband comes home?'

HYPOCHONDRIA

All sorts of bodily diseases are produced by half-used minds.
George Bernard Shaw

Contentment preserves one even from catching cold. Has a woman who knew that she was well dressed ever caught a cold? – No, not even when she had scarcely a rag to her back.
Friedrich Wilhelm Nietzsche

HYPOCRISY

Hypocrisy is the most difficult and nerve-racking vice that any man can pursue; it needs an unceasing vigilance and a rare detachment of spirit. It cannot, like adultery or gluttony, be practised in spare moments; it is a whole time job.
W. Somerset Maugham, Cakes and Ale, 1930

Hypocrisy is the only evil that walks invisible.
John Milton, (1608-1674)

A hypocrite combines the smooth appearance of virtue with the solid satisfaction of vice.
C. E. M. Joad (1891-1953), British author and academic

No man is a hypocrite in his pleasure.
Dr Samuel Johnson

Hypocrisy is the homage paid by vice to virtue.
Duc de la Rochefoucauld, Maximes

Virtue consisted in avoiding scandal and venereal disease.
Robert Cecil, British writer, *Life in Edwardian England,* 1969

IDEALISM

When they come downstairs from their ivory towers, idealists are apt to walk straight into the gutter.
Logan Pearsall Smith (1865-1946), American essayist

Idealism increases in direct proportion to one's distance from the problem.
John Galsworthy (1867-1933)

The idealist walks on tiptoe, the materialist on his heels.
Malcolm de Chazai, French writer

An idealist is a person who helps other people to be prosperous.
Henry Ford

We are all in the gutter, but some of us are looking at the stars.
Oscar Wilde

A man gazing at the stars is proverbially at the mercy of the puddles in the road.
Alexander Smith (1830-1867), Scottish poet

IDLENESS

A loafer always has the correct time.
Kin Hubbard (1868-1930), American humorist and journalist

I look upon indolence as a sort of suicide; for the man is effectually destroyed, though the appetites of the brute may survive.
Lord Chesterfield (1694-1773), English statesman, orator and wit

It is better to have loafed and lost than never to have loafed at all.
James Thurber (1894-1961) American humorist and illustrator

The insupportable labour of doing nothing.
Sir Richard Steel (1672-1729), English essayist, dramatist and editor

Idleness is an appendix to nobility.
Robert Burton (1577-1640), English clergyman and author

Lazy? He used to ride his bike over cobblestones to knock the ash off his ciggie.
Les Dawson, 1979

Well, we can't stand around here doing nothing, people will think we're workmen.
Spike Milligan, 1959

A good holiday is one spent among people whose notions of time are vaguer than yours.
J. B. Priestley

IMAGE

I called him Ernie because he's certainly no Rock.
Doris Day, of Rock Hudson

I've been around so long I can remember Doris Day before she was a virgin.
Groucho Marx

She is so pure, Moses couldn't even part her knees.
Joan Rivers, on Marie Osmond

Bambi with testosterone.
Owen Gleiberman, speaking about the singer, Prince

Elvis Presley had nothing to do with excellence, just myth.
Marlon Brando

Beauty has given me the chance not to be bitter, so I can be a better person . . . but I'm sick of supermodeldom – I don't want to be beautiful all the time.
Cindy Crawford, American supermodel

So many of us define ourselves by what we have, what we wear, what kind of house we live in and what kind of car we drive . . . if you think of yourself with a Cartier watch and a Hermes scarf, a house fire will destroy not only your possessions but your self.
Linda Henley, American writer

The one important thing I have learned over the years is the difference between taking one's work seriously and taking one's self seriously. The first is imperative and the second is disastrous.
Margot Fonteyn (1919-1991), English dancer

He attempts to achieve with his dress and platform manner what he cannot obtain through pure musical results.
Dennis Rooney, of violinist Nigel Kennedy

She is a piece of liquorice in shoes. She walks into a pool hall and they chalk her head.
Joan Rivers, of singer Diana Ross

Because we at Virgin have an image to keep up and we only like to hire young thin men and women.
Spokeswoman for Virgin Airlines, when asked why they liked to hire the young and thin

IMMORALITY

I like the English. They have the most rigid code of immorality in the world.
Malcolm Bradbury, British academic and novelist, *Eating People is Wrong*

Sex has become one of the most discussed subjects of modern times. The Victorians pretended it did not exist; the moderns pretend that nothing else exists.
Archbishop Fulton J. Sheen

B.B. on the screen is not simply a selfish delinquent. She has freshness, charm and a touch of mischievousness. She is irresponsible and immoral, but not deliberately cruel.
Observer, of French actress Brigitte Bardot, 1959

IMPOTENCE

The President is weak. When a man is impotent, his girlfriend goes off with another man. In the same way the country now has to find a new president, a strong one.
Vladimir Zhirinovsky, leader of the Russian nationalist party, of Boris Yeltsin

Thou Treacherous, base deserter of my
      flame,
False to my passion, fate to my fame,
      Through
what mistaken magic dost
      thou prove
So true to lewdness, so untrue to
      love.
John Wilmot, Earl of Rochester (1647-1680), English
courtier and poet

I told my wife that there was a chance that
radiation might hurt my reproductive organs but
she said in her opinion it's a small price to pay.
Johnny Carson

INDIFFERENCE

I regard you with an indifference closely bordering
on aversion.
Robert Louis Stevenson (1850-1894)

Lukewarmness I account a sin as great in love as
in religion.
Abraham Cowley (1618-1667), English author

INERTIA

When a man hasn't a good reason for doing a
thing, he has a good reason for letting it alone.
Sir Walter Scott (1771-1832)

Fixed like a plant on his peculiar spot,
To draw nutrition, propagate, and rot.
Alexander Pope (1688-1744)

INFATUATION

Infatuation is when you think that he's as sexy as Robert Redford, as smart as Henry Kissinger, as noble as Ralph Nader, as funny as Woody Allen and as athletic as Jimmy Connors. Love is when you realize that he's as sexy as Woody Allen, as smart as Jimmy Connors, as funny as Ralph Nader, as athletic as Henry Kissinger and nothing like Robert Redford – but you'll take him anyway.
Judith Viorst

When President Gorbachev came to Britain and she [Margaret Thatcher] showed him round the House, she positively glowed. Her skin turned pink, her eyes sparkled, she looked 20 years younger. She was clearly potty about him. Suddenly, her famous remark: 'Here is a man I could do business with', took on a whole new meaning.
Teresa Gorman, MP

INFIDELITY

Executive Mistress's Influence Mounting in US Boardrooms . . . Who is she? The executive mistress, that important figure found standing behind so many top executives and kneeling in front of still more.
Off the Wall Street Journal, 1982

Stan Waltz has decided to take unto himself a wife, but he hasn't decided yet whose . . .
Peter de Vries, Let Me Count the Ways, 1965

Those who are faithful know only the trivial side of love: it is the faithless who know love's tragedies.
Oscar Wilde, The Picture of Dorian Gray

I couldn't stand hearing her twitter on about her idyllic marriage.
Sarah Johnson, of Jilly Cooper, when Sarah revealed her affair with Jilly Cooper's husband

Young men want to be faithful, and are not; old men want to be faithless, and cannot.
Oscar Wilde, *The Picture of Dorian Gray*

Reading someone else's newspaper is like sleeping with someone else's wife. Nothing seems to be precisely in the right place, and when you find what you are looking for, it is not clear then how to respond to it.
Malcolm Bradbury, *Stepping Westward,* 1975

I've been in love with the same woman for forty-one years. If my wife finds out, she'll kill me.
Henny Youngman, 1970

But as any young woman engaging in her first infidelity knows, being willing is not quite the same as being able.
David Matza, writer, 1969

For us it is the confession that truth and sex are joined, through the obligatory and exhaustive expression of an individual secret.
Michel Foucault, writer, 1980

If your home burns down, rescue the dogs. At least they'll be faithful to you.
Lee Marvin, American film star

I have always held that it was a very good thing for a young girl to fall hopelessly in love with a married man so that, later on and in the opposite predicament, she could remember what an unassailable citadel a marriage can be.
Katherine Whitehorn

There is one thing I would break up over, and that is if she caught me with another woman. I won't stand for that.
Steve Martin, American actor and comedian

INFLATION

A double Scotch is about the size of a small Scotch before the war, and a single Scotch is nothing more than a dirty glass.
Lord Dundee, British politician

Americans are getting stronger. Twenty years ago, it took two people to carry 10 dollars' worth of groceries. Today, a five-year-old can do it.
Henny Youngman

I haven't heard of anybody who wants to stop living on account of the cost.
Kin Hubbard

INNOCENCE

Every harlot was a virgin once.
William Blake (1757-1827)

I used to be Snow White – but I drifted.
Mae West

Innocence ends when one is stripped of the delusion that one likes oneself.
Joan Didion, American writer

INSULTS

I won't eat anything that has intelligent life but I would gladly eat a network executive or a policeman.
Marty Feldman

. . . like being savaged by a dead sheep.
Denis Healey, on Geoffrey Howe

I treasure every moment that I do not see her.
Oscar Levant, on Phyllis Diller (attrib.)

So long as I am acting from duty and conviction, I am indifferent to taunts and jeers. I think they will probably do me more good than harm.
Sir Winston Churchill, 1945

There is no place in society for nasty-minded, rude people.
Peter Cook

It is easier to ridicule than commend.
Thomas Fuller (1608-1661), English clergyman and antiquary

If you can't say something good about someone, sit right here by me.
Alice Roosevelt Longworth, daughter of President Theodore Roosevelt. Embroidered on her favourite cushion

I succeed by saying what everyone else is thinking.
Joan Rivers, US comedienne and talk show host

He who slings mud generally loses ground.
Adlai Stevenson, 1954

INTERVIEWS

I'm notorious for giving a bad interview. I'm an actor, and I can't help but feel I'm boring when I'm on as myself.
Rock Hudson (1925-1985)

It is not every question that deserves an answer.
Publilius Syrus, Roman writer, 1st century BC

If I possessed the power of conveying unlimited
sexual attraction through the potency of my voice,
I would not be reduced to accepting a miserable
pittance from the BBC for interviewing a faded
female in a damp basement.
Gilbert Harding (1907-1960), British broadcaster on
being asked to sound more sexy when interviewing Mae
West

This woman is headstrong, obstinate and
dangerously self opinionated.
Report by the personnel officer, ICI, rejecting
Margaret Thatcher for a job, 1948

INTROSPECTION

When a man is wrapped up in himself he makes a
pretty small package.
John Ruskin (1819-1900), English critic

JAZZ

I'll play it first and tell you what it is later.
Miles Davis (1925-1991), Jazz musician

Jazz is the big brother of the blues. If a guy's
playing blues like we play, he's in high school.
When he starts playing jazz it's like going on to
college, to a school of higher learning.
B. B. King, blues guitarist

Jazz is the only music in which the same note can
be played night after night but differently each
time.
Ornette Coleman, jazz musician

Playing 'bop' is like playing Scrabble with all the
vowels missing.
Duke Ellington (1899-1974)

The performance is okay . . . but then Diamond
never attempts anything so difficult as chewing
gum and walking at the same time.
Rod McShane, writer and critic, of singer Neil Diamond
in *The Jazz Singer,* 1980

I saw him standing in snakeskin trousers with an electrified orange trumpet, playing a series of screeching notes that mean f*** all – I thought, why don't you just drive a red-hot nail through your balls?
Spike Milligan, comedian, of Miles Davis, 1988

Those whites can play instruments real fine. But there's something missing in their singing. They just don't eat enough pinto beans; they haven't had enough hard times.
Muddy Waters, musician

JEALOUSY

Never be possessive. If a female friend lets on that she is going out with another man, be kind and understanding. If she says she would like to go out with all the Dallas Cowboys, including the coaching staff, the same rule applies. Tell her: 'Kath, you just go right ahead and do what you feel is right.' Unless you actually care for her, in which case you must see to it that she has no male contact whatsoever.
Bruce Jay Friedman, *Sex and the Lonely Guy*, 1977

To jealousy, nothing is more frightful than laughter.
Francoise Sagan

I can be bitchy, yes. I am a jealous person; it's as simple as that.
Naomi Campbell, model

He was a man of strong passions, and the green-eyed monster ran up his leg and bit him on the bone.
P. G. Wodehouse, *Full Moon*, 1947

Glamour cannot exist without personal social envy being a common and widespread emotion.
John Berger, British critic

Envy is a kind of praise.
John Gay (1685-1732), English playwright

If someone with whom one is having an affair keeps on mentioning some woman whom he knew in the past, however long ago it is since they separated, one is always irritated.
The Pillow-Book of Sei Shongon, 10th century

There is always inequality in life. Some men are killed in a war and some men are wounded and some men never leave the country. Life is unfair.
John F. Kennedy (1917-1963)

K I S S I N G

It takes a lot of experience for a girl to kiss like a beginner.
Ladies' Home Journal, 1948

. . . we did one of those quick, awkward kisses where each of you gets a nose in the eye.
Clive James, Unreliable Memoirs, 1980

What lies lurk in kisses.
Heinrich Heine (1797-1856), German poet and journalist

A kiss can be a comma, a question mark or an exclamation point. That's basic spelling that every woman ought to know.
Mistinguett (1873-1956), French dancer and singer

Everybody winds up kissing the wrong person good night.
Andy Warhol (1928-1987), American artist and film-maker

The sound of a kiss is not so loud as that of a cannon, but its echo lasts a great deal longer.
Dr Oliver Wendell Holmes

Anyone who's a great kisser, I'm *always* interested in.
Cher, American actress and singer

. . . A man should kiss his wife's navel every day.
Nell Kimball (1854-1934), American madam and writer

There's absolutely an art to it. You have to think it's as good as what's coming later.
Kim Basinger

It becomes a bore – love scenes, kissing scenes. I prefer to fight.
Alain Delon

I'm fond of kissing. It's part of my job. God sent me down to kiss a lot of people.
Carrie Fisher

You think Cairo was upset? You should've seen the letter from my Aunt Rose!
Barbra Streisand on kissing Egyptian Omar Sharif in *Funny Girl*

I'm going to give you only one lip when we kiss. Because if I give you two, you'll never live through it.
Woody Allen, to co-star Michel Piccoli, on the set of *The Front*

L I E S

A lie can be half-way round the world before the truth has got its boots on.
James Callaghan

A little inaccuracy sometimes saves tons of explanation.
Saki (H. H. Munro), The Square Egg, 1924

I was brought up in a clergyman's household, so I am a first-class liar.
Dame Sybil Thorndike

You lie to two people in your life; your girlfriend and the police. Everyone else you tell the truth.
Jack Nicholson, American actor, reveals the secret of his success with women

L O N E L I N E S S

If there's anything worse than a woman living alone, it's a woman saying she likes it.
Stanley Shapiro and Maurice Richlin, Pillow Talk, 1959

When so many are lonely as seem to be lonely, it would be inexcusably selfish to be lonely alone.
Tennessee Williams, Camino Real, 1953

On stage I make love to 25,000 people; then I go home alone.
Janis Joplin (1943-1970), American singer

If I'm such a legend, then why am I so lonely? If I'm such a legend, then why do I sit at home for hours staring at the damned telephone, hoping it's out of order, even calling the operator asking her if she's *sure* it's not out of order.
Judy Garland (1922-1969)

Do not think that the solution to a man's solitude is a line of men masturbating and a line of women masturbating.
Lina Wertmuller, Italian film director

L O V E

Love is what you feel for a dog or a pussycat. It doesn't apply to humans.
Johnny Rotten, aka John Lydon

A grave mental disease.
Plato

A narcissism shared by two.
Rita Mae Brown

Greater love than this, he said, no man hath that a man lay down his wife for a friend. Go thou and do likewise. Thus, or words to that effect, said Zarathustra, sometime regius professor of French letters to the University of Oxtail.
James Joyce (1882-1941), Irish novelist and poet, Ulysses

Many a man has fallen in love with a girl in a light so dim he would not have chosen a suit by it.
Maurice Chevalier (1888-1972), French singer and actor (attrib. 1955)

It is very rarely that a man loves. And when he does it is nearly always fatal.
Hugh MacDiarmid (1892-1978) Scottish poet, *The International Brigade*

Love ceases to be a pleasure, when it ceases to be a secret.
Aphra Behn (1640-1689), English novelist and dramatist, *The Lover's Watch*

Once a woman has given you her heart, you can never get rid of the rest of her.
John Vanbrugh, *The Relapse*, 1696

I love her deeply. The trouble is it takes me a long time to tell her this.
Paulo Baron, who defrauded British Telecom out of £44,586 by phoning his girlfriend in Brazil, 1994

The drug which makes sexuality palatable in popular mythology.
Germaine Greer

I love the bitch to death.
Keith Richards, musician, of his wife.

Desperate madness.
John Ford, film director

Love is two minutes 52 seconds of squishing noises. It shows your mind isn't clicking right.
Johnny Rotten

Perhaps at 14 every boy should be in love with some ideal woman to put on a pedestal and worship. As he grows up, of course, he will put her on a pedestal the better to view her legs.
Barry Norman, British cinema critic and broadcaster

If only one could tell true love from false love as one can tell mushrooms from toadstools.
Katherine Mansfield (1888-1923), English writer

Ideally, couples need three lives; one for him, one for her, and one for them together.
Jacqueline Bisset, English actress

Love is a fire. But whether it is going to warm your hearth or burn down your house, you can never tell.
Joan Crawford (1906-1977), American actress

Age does not protect you from love. But love, to some extent, protects you from age.
Jeanne Moreau, French actress

Just another four letter word.
Tennessee Williams

Love is so much better when you are not married.
Maria Callas (1923-1977), opera singer

I love Mickey Mouse more than any woman I've every known.
Walt Disney

Never forget that the most powerful force on earth is love.
Nelson Rockefeller (1908-1979), to Henry Kissinger

What's love got to do with it? What's Ike got to do with it?
Ike Turner, Tina Turner's former husband

I love her, but her oars aren't touching the water these days.
Dean Martin, of actress Shirley MacLaine

Love, love, love – all the wretched cant of it, masking egotism, lust, masochism, fantasy, under a mythology of sentimental postures.
Germaine Greer

Because women can do nothing except love, they've given it a ridiculous importance.
W. Somerset Maugham (1874-1965), British novelist, *The Moon and Sixpence,* 1919

Man's love is of man's life a thing apart,
'Tis woman's whole existence.
Lord Byron, Don Juan

To men, love is an incident; to woman a vocation. They live by and for their emotions.
Denis Diderot, *Celibate's Apology*

If love is the answer,
Could you please rephrase the question?
Lily Tomlin, comedienne

Love is blind – and your cane is pink.
Serge Gainsbourg (1928-1991)

I have a love interest in every one of my films – a gun.
Arnold Schwarzenegger

The only thing I love in love is all of the feelings, the imaginations, the orgasms of the woman. For this reason I am not a good libertine.
Roger Vadim

L O V E R S

Imparadised in one another's arms.
John Milton

We that are true lovers run into strange capers.
Touchstone, *As You Like it,* William Shakespeare

A lover is someone who gives as much consideration to your warts as you do, and continues to admire you as you do. Many love affairs are simply servings of self-pity for two.
Alan Brien, British novelist and journalist

Every man wants a woman to appeal to his better side, his nobler instincts and his higher nature – and another woman to help him forget them.
Helen Rowland (1875-1950), American journalist

A mistress should be like a little country retreat near the town; not to dwell in constantly, but only for a night and away.
William Wycherley (1640-1716), English dramatist

Love ceases to be a pleasure when it ceases to be a secret.
Aphra Behn (1640-1689), English playwright and poet

A lover without indiscretion is no lover at all.
Thomas Hardy (1840-1928)

The difference is wide that the sheets will not decide.
Proverb

There are few people who are not ashamed of their love affairs when the infatuation is over.
Francois, duc de la Rochefoucauld

Scratch a lover and find a foe.
Dorothy Parker

I'm glad you like my Catherine. I like her too. She ruled thirty million people and had three thousand lovers. I do the best I can in two hours.
Mae West (1892-1980), US actress, speech from the stage after her performance in *Catherine the Great*

One can be a soldier without dying, and a lover without sighing.
Edwin Arnold (1832-1904), British poet

All mankind loves a lover.
Ralph Waldo Emerson (1803-1892), American poet and essayist, *Love, c.*1840

'Tis strange what a man may do, and a woman yet think him an angel.
William Makepeace Thackery (1811-1863), British novelist

Responses by *Sally Burton,* writer and widow of actor Richard Burton, when asked to comment on a number of men often quoted in the media as being good lovers . . .

He's that rare creature – a man's man and a woman's man.
of *Michael Caine,* British actor

Irresistible old reprobate. Each new woman mounts a rescue mission. But he's long gone.
of *Jeffrey Bernard,* British writer

Have a wife, have mistresses, call yourself a hero; thousands do. At least this one is honest and enthusiastic.
of *Alan Clark,* former defence minister

LUST

She gave me a smile I could feel in my hip pocket.
Raymond Chandler (1888-1959), US novelist, *Farewell, My Lovely,* 1940

All witchcraft comes from carnal lust which in woman is insatiable.
Jacob Sprenger and Hendrich Kramer, German Dominican monks, 1489

Latins are tenderly enthusiastic. In Brazil they throw flowers at you. In Argentina they throw themselves.
Marlene Dietrich (1904-1993), German-born film star

What is commonly called love; namely the desire of satisfying a voracious appetite with a certain quantity of delicate white human flesh.
Henry Fielding (1707-1754), British novelist

The trouble with life is that there are so many beautiful women and so little time.
John Barrymore (1882-1942), American actor

He is every woman's man and every man's woman.
Gaius Scribonius Curio, Roman consul, of Julius Caesar

I have looked on a lot of women with lust. I've committed adultery in my heart many times. God recognises I will do this and forgives me.
Jimmy Carter, US statesman and President

People will insist . . . on treating the mons Veneris as though it were Mount Everest.
Aldous Huxley (1894-1963)

What most men desire is a virgin who is a whore.
Edward Dahilberg, American author

Abstinence sows sand all over
   The ruddy limbs and flaming hair,
But desire gratified
   Plants fruits of life and beauty there.
William Blake (1757-1827)

We have two tyrannous physical passions;
concupiscence and chastity. We become mad in
pursuit of sex: we become equally mad in the
persecution of that pursuit.
George Bernard Shaw

Those who restrain Desire, do so because theirs is
weak enough to be restrained.
William Blake (1757-1827), British poet

I don't believe most women are as quickly or as
indiscriminately aroused as most men are. It's a
peculiar male problem to want to copulate with
almost anything that moves.
Roy Scheider

LYING

A little inaccuracy sometimes saves tons of
explanation.
Saki (1870-1916), Scottish author

Women lie about their age; men about their
income.
William Feather, American businessman

The best liar is he who makes the smallest amount
of lying to go the longest way.
Samuel Butler (1835-1902), English author

If you are going to lie, you go to jail for the lie
rather than the crime, so believe me, don't ever lie.
Richard Nixon, to John Dean III, due to testify before
Watergate Committee, 1973

When I make a mistake every one can see it, but
not when I lie.
Johann Wolfgang von Goethe (1749-1832)

The cruellest lies are often told in silence.
Robert Louis Stevenson

He will lie even when it is inconvenient, the sign of
the true artist.
Gore Vidal

It is hard to believe that a man is telling the truth when you know that you would lie if you were in his place.
H. L. Mencken

MARRIAGE

Hah! I always knew Frank would end up in bed with a boy!
Ava Gardner, actress, on the marriage of Frank Sinatra to Mia Farrow.

There are four stages to a marriage. First there's the affair, then the marriage, then children and finally the fourth stage, without which you cannot know a woman, the divorce.
Norman Mailer

My wife and I tried to breakfast together, but we had to stop or our marriage would have been wrecked.
Winston Churchill

Marriage is a great institution, but I'm not ready for an institution, yet.
Mae West

Marriage is a wonderful invention; but then again, so is a bicycle repair kit.
Billy Connolly, Scottish comedian and actor

Marriage, n. The state or condition of a community consisting of a master, a mistress and two slaves, making in all two.
Ambrose Bierce, The Devil's Dictionary

It destroys one's nerves to be amiable every day to the same human being.
Benjamin Disraeli

Marriage is a mistake every man should make.
Sir George Jessel (1824-1883), English judge

The most happy marriage I can picture or imagine to myself would be the union of a deaf man to a blind woman.
Samuel Taylor Coleridge (1772-1834), British poet, *Recollections, Allsop,* 1834

The trouble with my wife is that she is a whore in the kitchen and a cook in bed.
Geoffrey Gorer (1905-1985), British writer and anthropologist, *Exploring the English Character*, 1955

Whenever you want to marry someone, go have lunch with his ex-wife.
Shelley Winters, American actress

Sometimes I wonder if men and women really suit each other. Perhaps they should live next door and just visit now and then.
Katharine Hepburn, American actress

Marrying a man is like buying something you've been admiring for a long time in a shop window. You may love it when you get it home, but it doesn't always go with everything else.
Jean Kerr, American playwright

So that ends my first experience with matrimony, which I always thought a highly over-rated performance.
Isadora Duncan, US dancer, educator and writer

Bigamy is having one wife too many. Monogamy is the same thing.
Anon

When you're young, you think of marriage as a train you simply have to catch. You run and run until you've caught it and then you sit back and look out the window and realise you're bored.
Elizabeth Bowen (1899-1973), interview printed in the *Sunday Times*, 1988

The trouble with some women is they get all excited about nothing – then marry him.
Cher

Men who have a pierced ear are better prepared for marriage – they've experienced pain and bought jewellery.
Rita Rudner, American comedienne

MARTYRDOM

. . . a thing is not necessarily true because a man dies for it.
Oscar Wilde, *The Portrait of Mr. W.H.,* 1889

Martyrdom is the only way in which a man can become famous without ability.
George Bernard Shaw, *Essays in Fabian Socialism,* 1908

It is the cause, not the death, that makes the martyr.
Napoleon Bonaparte (1769-1821)

A cause may be inconvenient, but it's magnificent. It's like champagne or high shoes, and one must be prepared to suffer for it.
Arnold Bennett (1867-1931)

Martyrdom is an unnecessary complication to a first-rate mind.
Stephen Winsten (fl 1946-1951)

Women in drudgery knew
They must be one of four:
Whores, artists, saints, and wives.
Muriel Rukeyser (1913-1980), US poet, *Beast in View, Wreath of Women,* 1944

MASTURBATION

Don't knock it, it's sex with someone you love.
Woody Allen

Masturbation: the primary sexual activity of mankind. In the nineteenth century, it was a disease, in the twentieth, it's a cure.
Thomas Szasz, American psychiatrist

Writers are the most masturbatory of creatures. Ask any writer – they're like monkeys.
Anthony Burgess, writer

The difference between directing yourself and being directed is the difference between masturbation and making love.
Warren Beatty

MEANNESS

They asked Jack Benny if he would do something for the Actor's Orphanage – so he shot both his parents and moved in.
Bob Hope

It was said of old Sarah, Duchess of Marlborough, that she never puts dots over her i's, to save ink.
Horace Walpole (1717-1797), English author

There are many things that we would throw away, if we were not afraid that others might pick them up.
Oscar Wilde

MEN

Whenever I date a guy, I think, is this the man I want my children to spend their weekends with?
Rita Rudner, American comedienne

Men are creatures with two legs and eight hands.
Jayne Mansfield (1933-1967), American actress

Men are just little boys – but luckily not all over.
Jerry Hall, model, remark to Mick Jagger, Oxford University Union debate, 1993

A man is by nature a sexual animal. I've always had my special pets.
Mae West

A woman without a man is like a fish without a bicycle.
Gloria Steinem, American feminist and writer

Personally, I think if a woman hasn't met the right man by the time she's 24, she may be lucky.
Deborah Kerr, Scottish-born American actress

Show me a woman who doesn't feel guilty and I'll show you a man.
Erica Jong

Man forgives woman anything save the wit to outwit him.
Minna Antrim, Irish writer, 19th Century

I don't believe man is woman's natural enemy. Perhaps his lawyer is.
Shana Alexander, American writer

I live by a man's code, designed to fit a man's world, yet at the same time I never forget that a woman's first job is to choose the right shade of lipstick.
Carole Lombard (1908-1942), American actress

I require only three things in a man: he must be handsome, ruthless and stupid.
Dorothy Parker

Men are beasts and even beasts don't behave as they do.
Brigitte Bardot

I only like two kinds of men: domestic and imported.
Mae West

The male sex, as a sex, does not universally appeal to me. I find the men today less manly; but a woman of my age is not in a position to know exactly how manly they are.
Katharine Hepburn, American film star

I like men to behave like men – strong and childish.
Francoise Sagan, French novelist

However much men say sex is not on their minds all the time, it is – most of the time.
Jackie Collins, novelist

I truly believe I can be content only with a man who's a little crazy.
Elizabeth Taylor, film star and writer, *Elizabeth Takes Off*

One hell of an outlay for a very small return with most of them.
Glenda Jackson, British actress, politician

No nice men are good at getting taxis.
Katherine Whitehorn, columnist

Never trust a man who, when he's alone in a room with a tea cosy doesn't try it on.
Billy Connolly, Scottish actor and comedian

MISOGYNY

And remember, there's nothing these women won't do to satisfy
Their ever-moist groins; they've just one obsession
– sex.
Juvenal (60-130AD), Roman satirist, *Satires X*

God created woman. And boredom did indeed cease from that moment – but many other things ceased as well! Woman was God's *second* mistake.
Friedrich Wilhelm Nietzsche (1844-1900), German philosopher, *The Antichrist*, 1895

You will find that the woman who is really kind to dogs is always one who has failed to inspire sympathy in men.
Max Beerbohm (1872-1956), British writer, *Zuleika Dobson*, 1911

Of all the plagues with which the world is curst,
Of every ill, a woman is the worst.
George Granville (1667-1735), British poet and dramatist, *The British Enchanters*

I expect that Woman will be the last thing civilized by man.
George Meredith (1828-1909), British novelist, *The Ordeal of Richard Feverel*, 1859

Brigands demand your money or your life; women require both.
Samuel Butler (1612-1680), English satirist (attrib. 1680)

A smart girl is one who knows how to play tennis, piano and dumb.
Lynn Redgrave, British actress

MIDDLE AGE

I have everything now I had 20 years ago – except now it's all lower.
Gypsy Rose Lee, 1968

Middle age is when, wherever you go on holiday, you pack a sweater.
Denis Norden

There are no old men any more. *Playboy* and *Penthouse* have between them made an ideal of eternal adolescence, sunburnt and saunaed, with the grey dorianed out of it.
Peter Ustinov, *Dear Me*

Years ago we discovered the exact point, the dead centre of middle age. It occurs when you are too young to take up golf and too old to rush up to the net.
Franklin P. Adams, *Nods and Becks,* 1944

My forties are the best time I have ever gone through.
Elizabeth Taylor

The only really frightening thing about middle age is the knowledge that you'll grow out of it.
Doris Day

I'm so bitter . . . they've suddenly made me feel middle-aged.
Isabella Rossellini, film actress, dropped by *Lancome* allegedly because at 41, she's too old, 1994

La Pasionara of middle-age privilege.
Denis Healey, of Margaret Thatcher

A lady of a 'certain age', which means Certainly aged.
Lord Byron, *Don Juan*

I refuse to admit that I am more than 52, even if that does make my sons illegitimate.
Nancy Astor, US born, British politician, 1964 (attrib.)

She may very well pass for 43 in the dusk, with a light behind her!
W. S. Gilbert (1836-1911), British dramatist, *Trial By Jury,* 1875

I'm a woman who has undoubtedly made a success of her career but not of her life. The myth of Bardot is finished, but Brigitte is me.
Brigitte Bardot, said on her 40th birthday

One searches the magazines in vain for women past their first youth. The middle-aged face apparently sells neither perfume nor floor wax. The role of the mature woman in the media is almost entirely negative.
Janet Harris, US writer and educator, *The Prime of Ms America,* 1975

At my age I've come to the conclusion that women are really coming into their own and they're at their best when they've passed 40.
Clint Eastwood

Age has mental pleasures to compensate. Of course, I regret sometimes the beautiful fresh bodies. But you can buy those in the market.
Franco Zeffirelli, film director

What happens during the climacteric is that the people she has served all her life stop making demands on her. She becomes a moon without an earth. What she wants is to be wanted and nobody wants her.
Germaine Greer, Australian born British writer and feminist, *The Change,* 1991

Joan Collins career is a testimony to menopausal chic.
Erica Jong, writer

MISTAKES

Nowadays most people die of a sort of creeping common sense, and discover when it is too late that the only things one never regrets are one's mistakes.
Oscar Wilde, The Picture of Dorian Gray, 1891

Whenever a man does a thoroughly stupid thing, it is always from the noblest of motives.
Oscar Wilde, The Picture of Dorian Gray

If only one could have two lives; the first in which to make one's mistakes, which seem as if they have to be made; and the second in which to profit by them.
D. H. Lawrence, 1962

You know, by the time you reach my age, you've made plenty of mistakes if you've lived your life properly.
Ronald Reagan, 1987

The physician can bury his mistakes, but the architect can only advise his clients to plant vines.
Frank Lloyd Wright (1869-1959), US architect

MISTRESSES

Music is my mistress and she plays second fiddle to no one.
Duke Ellington, jazz musician

Buy old masters. They fetch a better price than old mistresses.
Lord Beaverbrook, Canadian press magnate

I need several mistresses; if I had only one, she's be dead inside eight days.
Alexander Dumas

... If you want to be a political mistress, everything you have done to date spells disaster. Discretion has to be the key for political dalliances, and the second-worst crime is to be found out, having your name in the newspapers and bring about the resignation of the politician concerned.
Julia Langdon, British writer and journalist

She is every man's fantasy mistress. She gave you the impression that, if your imagination had to sin, it could at least congratulate itself on its impeccable taste.
Alistair Cooke, British journalist, of Mae West

Of course, I will underscore the values of the family. But I will also not neglect to mention that in my recent personal life I have felt how these values can be endangered.
Thomas Klestil, President of Austria, remarking about his approach to United Nations speech, facing calls for his resignation after announcing his affair with an aide

I cannot say why he [Steve Norris, MP] sold it. But I've read about his private life, and I know women are expensive!
Jean-Louis Lagadou, estate agent, speculating on why Norris sold his house in Provence

I forgot the others. Honestly, that's all it is. I didn't realise people normally list all their marriages. You might as well list mistresses.
Terence Conran, designer, on why he mentioned only his third wife in *Who's Who?*

MONEY

If you can count your money then you are not really a rich man.
Paul Getty

Money is better than poverty, if only for financial reasons.
Woody Allen, Without Feathers, 1972

Money can't buy friends but you can get a better class of enemy.
Spike Milligan, Puckoon, 1963

I don't want money. It is only people who pay their bills who want that, and I never pay mine.
Oscar Wilde, The Picture of Dorian Gray, 1891

Money, it turned out, was exactly like sex; you thought of nothing else if you didn't have it and thought of other things if you did.
James Baldwin (1927-1987), US writer, *Nobody Knows My Name*

She mentioned I was important to her. That's very satisfying, but a cheque would be better.
Deborah Harry, singer, on Madonna

All right, I like spending money! But name one other extravagance!
Max Kauffmann

She didn't get that terrific body from exercise. She got it from lifting all that money.
Joan Rivers, of actress Jane Fonda, 1987

Did you ever hear of a kid playing accountant – even if he wanted to be one?
Jackie Mason, comedian, 1969

Making money is pretty pointless and it needs constant attention.
Adam Faith, singer and actor

As Chancellor Lamont came in for a fraternal drink with Labour's John Smith and Gordon Brown, a group of Labour MPs' lusty singing broke off in mid verse and launched into 'Hey Big Spender'. Norman Lamont, I am happy to say, took it all exceptionally well.
The Mail on Sunday, 1992

They gave me star treatment because I was making a lot of money. But I was just as good when I was poor.
Bob Marley (1945-1981), Jamaican reggae singer, 1981

Being a Yorkshire person has made me tough and resilient. I am also quite smart about money.
Barbara Taylor Bradford, author

I don't know how much money I've got . . . I did ask the accountant how much it came to. I wrote it down on a bit of paper. But I've lost the bit of paper.
John Lennon (1940-1980), British rock musician, to Hunter Davies

The rich hate signing cheques. Hence the success of credit cards.
Graham Greene, British novelist, *Dr Fischer of Geneva*

MURDER

If the desire to kill and the opportunity to kill came always together, who would escape hanging?
Mark Twain

Murder is always a mistake . . . One should never do anything that one cannot talk about after dinner.
Oscar Wilde, *The Picture of Dorian Gray*

Every murderer is probably somebody's old friend.
Agatha Christie (1891-1976)

MOTHERS-IN-LAW

My mother-in-law broke up my marriage. My wife came home from work one day and found me in bed with her.
Lenny Bruce

I haven't spoken to my mother-in-law for 18 months – I don't like to interrupt her.
Ken Dodd

Behind every successful man stands a surprised mother-in-law.
Hubert Humphrey, 1964

The mother-in-law thinks I'm effeminate: not that I mind that because, beside her, I am!
Les Dawson (1940-1993)

Honolulu – it's got everything. Sand for the children, sun for the wife, sharks for the wife's mother.
Ken Dodd

M U S I C

The only sensual pleasure without vice.
Samuel Johnson, referring to music, *Johnsonian Miscellanies*

This instrument is how I met every woman in my life – it wasn't this face.
Billy Joel, American musician

Popular music in the USA is one of the few things in the twentieth century that have made giant strides in reverse.
Bing Crosby

Three farts and a raspberry, orchestrated.
John Barbirolli, conductor, his opinion of modern music

The chief objection to playing wind instruments is that it prolongs the life of the player.
George Bernard Shaw

I've got to try the bagpipes. It's like trying to blow an octopus.
James Galway, flautist

I can sing as well as Fred Astaire can act.
Burt Reynolds, American actor

Most of all he gives the impression of being a spoilt child. I am very near to detesting him as a composer.
Clara Schumann, of Franz Liszt, 1841

Few people know that the CIA are planning to cripple Iran by playing this album (*ESP*) on special loudspeakers secretly parachuted into the country.
Record Mirror of the Bee Gees latest album, 1988

I like Wagner's music better than anybody's. It is so loud that one can talk the whole time without people hearing what one says.
Oscar Wilde, on Richard Wagner

Opera is people singing when they should be talking.
The Mail on Sunday, 1992

In the final analysis, opera is a poor substitute for baseball.
Los Angeles Herald, 1986

I lost all my friends in the Bay City Rollers disaster of '74; it was like some plague, a complete wipe-out . . . from their moronic prancing and chanting, from their gormless unformed Pools-winner faces, from their tartan trimmings and short pants.
Julie Burchill, of the group *The Bay City Rollers*

Whoever is doing the Bay City Rollers' publicity has no sense of shame.
John Peel, Radio 1

A little glimpse into hell.
Kenneth Tynan, of Gerry and the Pacemakers movie *Ferry Cross the Mersey,* 1964

Remember the Time when you used to make decent f***ing records?
Melody Maker, referring to Michael Jackson's *Remember the Time.*

Those whites can play instruments real fine. But there's something missing in their singing. They just don't eat enough pinto beans; they haven't had enough hard times.
Muddy Waters, musician

N A R C I S S I S M

He fell in love with himself at first sight and it is a passion to which he has always remained faithful. Self-love seems so often unrequited.
Anthony Powell, *The Acceptance World,* 1955

A narcissist is someone better looking than you are.
Gore Vidal

A fashionable woman is always in love – with herself.
Francois, duc de la Rochefoucauld

It is a great help for a man to be in love with himself. For an actor, however, it is absolutely essential.
Robert Morley, 1979

Some of the greatest affairs I've known involved one actor unassisted.
Wilson Mizner (1876-1933), American dramatist and wit (attrib.)

NEUROSIS

The psychotic person knows that two and two make five and is perfectly happy about it; the neurotic person knows that two and two make four, but is terribly worried about it.
Radio doctor, 1954

Everything great in the world comes from neurotics. They alone have found our religions and composed our masterpieces.
Marcel Proust (1871-1922)

Neurosis is always a substitute for legitimate suffering.
Carl Jung (1875-1961)

NEWSPAPERS

I love the weight of American Sunday newspapers. Pulling them up off the floor is good for the figure.
Noel Coward (attrib.)

People everywhere confuse
What they read in newspapers with news.
A. J. Liebling, New Yorker, 1956

Newspapers have become like evil little curtain-twitchers, crouching outside the gate to take dodgy pictures so they can write something catty.
Joanna Lumley, British actress

Early in life I had noticed that no event is ever correctly reported in a newspaper.
George Orwell

An editor is one who separates the wheat from the chaff and prints the chaff.
Adlai Stevenson

In the old days men had the rack, now they have the Press.
Oscar Wilde (1854-1900)

The Sunday papers are the same every week . . . those ghastly obligatory articles by women on how awful it is to be a woman.
Jeffrey Bernard

If I blow my nose they would say I'm trying to spread germ warfare.
Ken Livingstone, of *The Daily Mail*

Newspapers too thick, lavatory paper too thin.
Sir Winston Churchill, on his trip to New York

It is no surprise the *Sun* can cut its price. That's because it's a cut price comic. It insults the reader's intelligence.
David Banks, editor, *The Daily Mail,* 1993

The broads who work in the press are the hookers of the press. I might offer them a buck and a half.
Frank Sinatra

Libby is a walking women's page. She lives it. She writes about it. Then she charges VAT on it.
The Mail on Sunday, on Libby Purves, author and radio presenter

N I C E N E S S

The disease of niceness cripples more lives than alcoholism. Nice people are simply afraid to say no.
Robin Chandler, psychological trainer

N O S I N E S S

The idea of strictly minding our own business is mouldy rubbish. Who could be so selfish?
Myrtle Baker, American actress

N U D I T Y

The part never calls for it [nudity]. And I've never even used that excuse. The box office calls for it.
Helen Mirren, British actress, of her latest film

Oh yes, I had the radio on.
Marilyn Monroe, discussing a nude photograph of herself with a journalist who asked 'Didn't you have anything on?'

Whew, what a bony butt.
Michael Douglas, on seeing himself naked on screen

I wasn't really naked. I simply didn't have any clothes on.
Josephine Baker

I was appalled and naïve.
Dawn French, comic actress, talking of the coverage she got when she posed nude in a bid to prove big girls are desirable

I'm not *against* naked girls – not as often as I'd like to be.
Benny Hill, British comedian

I'm an interesting, shy and vulnerable woman. My husband has never seen me naked. Nor has he expressed the least desire to do so.
Dame Edna Everage, aka Barry Humphries, housewife and superstar

A funny thing is happening to nudity in the theatre; it's the men, not the women, who are taking their clothes off.
Charles Spencer, on the latest theatre fashion, 1994

There is an unseemly exposure of the mind, as well as of the body.
William Hazlitt (1778-1830), English essayist

Every young sculptor seems to think that he must give the world some specimen of indecorous womanhood, and call it Eve, Venus, a Nymph, or any name that may apologise for a lack of decent clothing.
Nathaniel Hawthorne (1804-1864), American novelist

Any Ophelia worth her salt would take off her dress when she went mad, and Lady Macbeth was often without a nightie.
Charles Spencer, on the latest theatre fashion, 1994

Full-frontal nudity . . . has now become accepted
by every branch of the theatrical profession with
the possible exception of lady accordion-players.
Denis Norden, *You Can't Have Your Kayak and Heat It,*
1973

OBESITY

Imprisoned in every fat man, a thin one is wildly
signalling to be let out.
Cyril Connolly (1903-1974), British critic

A big man has no time really to do anything but
just sit and be big.
F. Scott Fitzgerald (1896-1940)

I'm fat and proud of it. If someone asks me how
my diet is going, I say, 'Fine, how was your
lobotomy?'
Roseanne Arnold, American actress

It can actually be a lot of fun.
Helmut Kohl, German Chancellor, on his corpulence

Outside every fat man there is an even fatter man
trying to close in.
Kingsley Amis, British author

I told the doctor I had a terrible stomach problem.
She said: 'You have, it's bloody enormous.'
Jo Brand, comedienne

In Rochdale we've got Cyril Smith who's so fat he
takes up most of the f***ing town.
Lisa Stansfield, British singer, of MP Cyril Smith

I deliberately keep my weight up so that f***ers
like you won't fancy me.
Jo Brand, comedienne, to hecklers

We should have been alerted when a British
journalist submitted a feature on Roy Hattersley to
an American magazine and found that his
description of him as 'fat' had been changed to
'nutritionally challenged'.
Maurice Chittenden, on the spread of political
correctness

We are neither fattist nor elitist. Our policy is very clear. Like all airlines we employ cabin crew whose weight must be in proportion to their height.
Virgin Airlines spokesman, hitting back at allegations that it discriminated against fat people

Isn't it quite awful that a woman should let her figure go in this way?
John Junor, writer and columnist, of American actress, Tyne Daly

The temptation always is to put a fat body in a tent.
Vivienne Westwood, British designer

OBSCENITY

It's a heavy breather wanting to reverse the charges . . .
Marc, cartoon in *The Times,* 1973

Obscenity is what happens to shock some elderly and ignorant magistrate.
Bertrand Russell, Look, 1954

Obscenity can be found in every book except the telephone directory.
George Bernard Shaw

Obscenity is whatever gives a judge an erection.
Anon

I just want to go and be obscene in private with my friends.
Richard Neville, Australian journalist, on his release after the OZ magazine obscenity trial

ORGASM

An orgasm is just a reflex like a sneeze.
Dr Ruth Westheimer

I may not be a great actress but I've become the greatest at screen orgasms. Ten seconds of heavy breathing, roll your head from side to side, simulate a slight asthma attack and die a little.
Candice Bergen, American actress

When the ecstatic body grips
Its heaven, with little sobbing cries.
E. R. Dodds (1893-1979), British classical scholar

I finally had an orgasm . . . and my doctor told me it was the wrong kind.
Woody Allen, *Manhattan,* 1979

The truth is I thought I forgot how to do that.
Meg Ryan, American actress, receiving Harvard University's Hasty Pudding award. Ryan was handed a conductor's baton and led the audience through a re-enactment of a fake orgasm scene from the film *When Harry Met Sally*

In the case of some women, orgasms take a bit of time. Before signing on with a partner, make sure you are willing to lay aside, say, the month of June, with sandwiches having to be brought in.
Bruce Jay Friedman, American writer and humorist

ORGIES

If God had meant us to have group sex, I guess he'd have given us all more organs.
Malcolm Bradbury, British author

You get a better class of person at orgies, because people have to keep in trim more. There is an awful lot of going round holding in your stomach, you know. Everybody is very polite to each other. The conversation isn't very good but you can't have everything.
Gore Vidal

PARANOIA

Psychiatrist (to patient): You're suffering from paranoia. Anyone'll tell you.
Hector Breeze, cartoon in *Private Eye*

I told my psychiatrist that everyone hates me. He said I was being ridiculous – everyone hasn't met me yet.
Rodney Dangerfield

Even a paranoid can have enemies.
Henry Kissinger

PASSION

Some people lose control of their sluice gates of passion.
Worker's Daily, Beijing, 1981

The passions are the only orators which always persuade.
Francois, duc de La Rochefoucauld

It is with our passions as it is with fire and water, they are good servants, but bad masters.
Roger L'Estrange (1616-1704), English journalist and writer, *Aesop's Fables*

I've always admitted that I'm ruled by my passions.
Elizabeth Taylor

Be a good animal, true to your animal instincts.
D. H. Lawrence (1885-1930)

A really grand passion is comparatively rare nowadays. It is the privilege of people who have nothing to do. That is the one use of the idle classes in the country.
Oscar Wilde, A Woman of No Importance, 1893

The passion and starry-eyed joys of the honeymoon are but callow experiments in a search for the magnificent which lies beyond the horizon.
Barbara Cartland, British romantic novelist

No passion in the world is equal to the passion to alter someone else's draft.
H. G. Wells, author

Passion thrives on proximity and secrecy. And when passion and harmony combine, they are a heady cocktail.
Style and Travel, 1994

P E R V E R S I O N

Commit the oldest sins the newest kind of ways.
William Shakespeare (1564-1616), *King Henry IV*

Socialism is a filthy disgusting perversion.
We are the pure.
Speaker, Young Conservatives' conference

The human knee is a joint and not an entertainment.
Percy Hammond (1873-1936), American critic

. . . The last few weeks have told me that one person's sexual perversion is another's preferred sexual practice.
The idea that young people would be attracted to some middle-aged old piggy . . .
Edwina Currie, supporting the lowering of the age of consent for homosexual relations

Chastity – the most unnatural of the sexual perversions.
Aldous Huxley

Until the end of the 19th century, sexual pleasure was essentially associated with sin, and perversion embraced almost every non-procreative act from birth control to buggery.
The Observer, 1994

P E S S I M I S M

Life is divided into the horrible and the miserable.
Woody Allen and Marshall Brickman, *Annie Hall,* 1977

Things are going to get a lot worse before they get worse.
Lily Tomlin

A pessimist is one who has been intimately acquainted with an optimist.
Elbert Hubbard (1856-1915), American author

There is no sadder sight than a young pessimist.
Mark Twain

A pessimist is a man who thinks all women are bad. An optimist is one who hopes they are.
Chauncey Depew

Pessimists have already begun to worry about what is going to replace automation.
Laurence J. Peter

One has to have the courage of one's pessimism.
Ian McEwan, British author

PETTING

. . . [he] twisted my nipples as though tuning a radio.
Lisa Alther, *Kinflicks,* 1976

The requirements of romantic love are difficult to satisfy in the trunk of a Dodge Dart.
Lisa Alther, *Kinflicks,* 1976

Whoever called it necking was a poor judge of anatomy.
Groucho Marx

PLAGIARISM

Immature artists imitate. Mature artists steal.
Lionel Trilling (1905-1975), American literary critic

The only 'ism she believes in is plagiarism.
Dorothy Parker, of a woman writer (attrib.)

If you steal from one author, it's plagiarism; if you steal from many, it's research.
Wilson Mizner (1876-1933), American dramatist and wit

It is a mean thief, or a successful author, that plunders the dead.
Austin O'Malley (1858-1932), American occulist and author

Whatever is well said by another, is mine.
Seneca (5-65AD), Roman writer, philosopher and statesman

It's a wisecrack that knows its own father.
Raymond Clapper (1892-1944), American journalist

A man will turn over half a library to make one book.
Samuel Johnson, *Life of Johnson,* J. Boswell

PLASTIC SURGERY

She's silicone from the knees up.
George Masters, make-up artist, of Raquel Welch

I meet people I don't even recognise as who they used to be! I think men are foolish to go for this sort of surgery. I don't fear ageing ungracefully.
Clint Eastwood, American actor

'You're looking good – been on holiday?' If friends ask this question, it's proof of successful surgery.
A top plastic surgeon

POLITICS

What I don't understand is why a complete wimp like me keeps winning.
John Major, after the 1993 elections

I am proud to be called a pig. It stands for pride, integrity and guts.
Ronald Reagan

I would not like to be a Russian leader, they never know when they are being taped.
Richard Nixon

What satirist ever toppled the Government? Swift managed to get one small tax changed in his whole career.
Ian Hislop, editor of *Private Eye*

You don't need to tell deliberate lies; but sometimes you have to be evasive.
Margaret Thatcher

They see the House of Commons as a political soap opera, complete with its Dirty Dens, JRs and Kylie Minogues – good for entertainment, but not of much real relevance to their daily lives.
Paddy Ashdown, MP, on the public perception of politicians

I am a bit long in the tooth to become a stalking filly.
Teresa Gorman, ruling herself out as a stalking-horse candidate to challenge Prime Minister John Major

He means well. He just wants a bit of encouragement. Like the Prince of Wales.
Dame Barbara Cartland, speaking of John Major

When they circumcised Herbert Samuel, they threw away the wrong bit.
David Lloyd George (1863-1945), on his follow Liberal

POLITICAL CORRECTNESS

Political correctness is balls.
Whoopi Goldberg, American actress

The misnamed fashion for what people call 'political correctness' amounts to testing everything, every aspect of life, every aspect of society, against a pre-determined, pre-ordained view.
The Prince of Wales, 1994

PORNOGRAPHY

A Porn-again publicist . . . her reports are Masters and Johnson with a dab of perfume behind the labia.
Profile on Shere Hite

At last, an unprintable book that is readable.
Ezra Pound, of Henry Miller's *Tropic of Cancer,* 1934

I am not trying to claim porn as a worthwhile artistic genre. Pornography is obscene, debasing and disgraceful. The point is, so am I. I'm sorry.
David Baddiel, comedian and pornography consumer

The worst that can be said about pornography is that it leads not to 'anti-social' acts but to the reading of more pornography.
Gore Vidal, *Reflections upon a Sinking Ship,* 1969

Nine-tenths of the appeal of pornography is due to the indecent feelings concerning sex which moralists inculcate in the young; the other tenth is physiological, and will occur in one way or another whatever the state of the law may be.
Bertrand Russell

Obscenity is such a tiny kingdom that a single tour covers it completely.
Heywood Broun (1888-1939), American journalist and novelist

Pornography is the attempt to insult sex, to do dirt on it.
D. H. Lawrence

Yes, but Page Three is not pornography.
Samantha Fox, Page Three model, when asked if pornography degrades women

I don't remember making them, I was always stoned out of my mind.
Traci Lords, former porno film star

It's red hot mate. I hate to think of this sort of book getting into the wrong hands. As soon as I've finished this, I shall recommend they ban it.
Tony Hancock (1924-1968), British comedian, from script by Ray Galton and Alan Simpson

It'll be a sad day for sexual liberation when the pornography addict has to settle for the real thing.
Brendan Francis, writer and journalist

She is the pinup, the centrefold, the poster, the postcard, the dirty picture, naked, half dressed, laid out, legs spread, breast or ass protruding. She is the thing she is supposed to be; the thing that makes him erect.
Andrea Dworkin, American writer and journalist, *Pornography, Men Possessing Women,* 1981

I found the whole thing absurd. The idea of having sex five times with five different men before five past 11 does not turn me on in the slightest.
Comments of a reader asked to review a recently published sexually explicit novel, *The Observer,* 1994

My reaction to porno films is as follows: After the
first 10 minutes, I want to go home and screw.
After the first 20 minutes, I never want to go home
and screw.
Erica Jong

We have to compete with newspapers which have
double-page spreads of pubic hair.
Rupert Murdoch, publisher of *The Sun* and *The News
of the World,* justifying pin-ups in his newspapers

P O W E R

Power is the ultimate aphrodisiac.
Henry Kissinger

Power corrupts, but lack of power corrupts
absolutely.
Adlai Stevenson (1900-1965), American politician

The place doesn't just have a whiff, it is *drenched*
in the scent of power. People flock here from the
four corners of the world, people who shape
events, the movers and the shakers of the universe.
You can't help but be turned on by it.
Teresa Gorman, MP, talking about the Palace of
Westminster

Europe might well be better off if its finances were
looked after by the Swiss, its foreign policy by the
French, its business affairs by the Germans, its
sexual behaviour by the Italians. The great thing is
to remove all power from London.
Auberon Waugh, writer

The thing women have to learn is that nobody
gives you power. You just take it.
Roseanne Barr, comedienne

Too bad all the people who know how to run the
country are busy driving taxi cabs and cutting hair.
George Burns

PREJUDICES

Our prejudices are our mistresses; reason is at best our wife, very often needed, but seldom minded.
Lord Chesterfield (1694-1773), English statesman

A prejudice is a vagrant opinion without visible means of support.
Ambrose Bierce

A great many people think they are thinking when they are merely rearranging their prejudices.
William James (1842-1910), American psychologist and philosopher

The collection of prejudices which is called political philosophy is useful provided that it is not called philosophy.
Bertrand Russell

Common sense is the collection of prejudices acquired by age eighteen.
Albert Einstein

PRIDE

I was beaten up at school but now I'm proud of my faith.
Steven Spielberg, film director, revealing that taunts at school made him feel ashamed of being Jewish, *Daily Mail,* 1994

The one thing I will never do is change my appearance and live in a blonde wig in another country.
Salman Rushdie, writer

It was I who introduced bottled water into India.
Dame Barbara Cartland

I am a Ford, not a Lincoln . . . I am proud – very proud – to be one of 200 million Americans.
Gerald Ford, on becoming President, 1973

Of all the causes which conspire to blind
Man's erring judgment, and misguide the
mind.
What the weak head with strongest bias
rules,
is Pride, the never-failing vice of fools.
Alexander Pope

I am bursting with pride, which is why I have
absolutely no vanity.
Noel Coward

PROCRASTINATION

If a thing's worth doing, it's worth doing late.
Frederick Oliver, writer

Procrastination is the art of keeping up with
yesterday.
Don Marquis (1878-1937), American humorist and
journalist

Procrastination is the thief of time.
Edward Young (1683-1765), English poet

Don't put off till tomorrow what can be enjoyed
today.
Josh Billings (1818-1885), American humorist

If you're in the penalty area and aren't sure what
to do with the ball, just stick it in the net and we'll
discuss your options afterwards.
Bill Shankly (1913-1981), Scottish footballer and
manager

PROHIBITION

I am certain that the good Lord never intended
grapes to be made into jelly.
Fiorello La Guardia (1882-1947), American politician

The South is dry and will vote dry. That is,
everybody sober enough to stagger to the polls
will.
Will Rogers, Oklahoma City, 1926

Once, during Prohibition, I was forced to live for days on nothing but food and water.
W. C. Fields

PROMISCUITY

She's the original good time that was had by all.
Bette Davis, of another actress

The girl speaks 18 languages and can't say no in any of them.
Dorothy Parker, of a famous actress

What's a promiscuous person? It's usually someone who is getting more sex than you are.
Victor Lownes, writer

You were born with your legs apart. They'll send you to your grave in a Y-shaped coffin.
Joe Orton, What the Butler Saw, 1969

We still have these double standards where the emphasis is all on the male's sexual appetites – that it's OK for him to collect as many scalps as he can before he settles down and 'pays the price'. If a woman displays the same attitude, all the epithets that exist in the English language are laid at her door, and with extraordinary bitterness.
Glenda Jackson, English actress and MP

Permissiveness is simply removing the dust sheets from our follies.
Edna O'Brien, Irish author

It is absurd to say that a man can't love one woman all the time as it is to say that a violinist needs several violins to play the same piece of music.
Honore de Balzac (1799-1850)

I am not promiscuous, you know. Promiscuity implies that attraction is not necessary.
Tallulah Bankhead (1908-1968), American actress

PROSTITUTION

Prostitutes believe in marriage. It provides them with most of their trade.
Suzie, *Knave,* 1975

This is the virgin territory for whorehouses.
Al Capone (1899-1947), talking about Chicago *c.*1925

We're so busy because of the holiday weekend that we're literally all at it like rabbits.
Escort girl, describing how their Easter bunny costumes helped increase business

Prostitution gives her an opportunity to meet people. It provides fresh air and wholesome exercise, and it keep her out of trouble.
Joseph Heller, *Catch-22,* 1961

The big difference between sex for money and sex for free is that sex for money usually costs less.
Brendan Francis

107 MPs have paid 50,000 visits over 10 years.
Lindi St Clair, prostitute

I don't think a prostitute is more moral than a wife, but they do the same thing.
Prince Philip, the consort of Queen Elizabeth II, 1988

If a woman hasn't got a tiny streak of a harlot in her, she's a dry stick as a rule.
D. H. Lawrence (1855-1930)

Prisons are built with stones of Law,
Brothels with bricks of Religion.
William Blake (1757-1827)

No, just clap in Germany in a whirlpool bath with a hooker; the condom must have floated off in the bubbles.
Jim Davidson, English comedian, when asked if he sustained any war wounds entertaining the troops in the Falklands, Beirut, Croatia and Bosnia, 1994

PUNK

I can imagine him becoming a successful hairdresser, a singing Vidal Sassoon.
Malcolm McLaren, British rock impresario, of Johnny Rotten

Punks in their silly leather jackets are a cliché. I have never liked the term and have never discussed it. I just got on with it and got out of it when it became a competition.
John Lydon, formerly Johnny Rotten

PURITANISM

We have long passed the Victorian era, when asterisks were followed after a certain interval by a baby.
W. Somerset Maugham, The Constant Wife, 1926

Puritanism: the haunting fear that someone somewhere may be happy.
H. L. Mencken (1880-1956), American journalist and linguist, *Sententiae,* 1920

The prig is a very interesting psychological study, and though of all poses a moral pose is the most offensive, still to have a pose at all is something.
Oscar Wilde, The Critic as Artist, 1890

QUOTATIONS

In the dying world I come from, quotation is a national vice. It used to be the classics, now it's lyric verse.
Evelyn Waugh (1903-1966), British novelist

The surest way to make a monkey out of a man is to quote him.
Robert Benchley (1889-1945), American humorist and critic

I often quote myself. It adds spice to my conversation.
George Bernard Shaw (1856-1950)

R A N D Y

I cannot believe how randy I have become over the past three or four years. I'm much juicier now.
Dawn French, actress

R A P E

I strongly feel that a rapist is a rapist, whether he is married to his victim or not.
John Patten, British politician, commenting on the law ruling that a husband can be guilty of raping his wife

R E C E S S I O N

Most of us have stopped using silver every day.
Margaret Thatcher

These dark days will be worth all they cost us if they teach us that our true destiny is not to be ministered unto but to minster to ourselves and to our fellow men.
Franklin D. Roosevelt (1882-1945)

R E P U T A T I O N

I was never that raucous. You do one bad thing a year and it gets talked about for the rest of your life. That was the pattern of my naughtiness. I guess people took notice because I was supposed to be a young lady. If I'd been a guy, they'd have said it was normal.
Debra Winger, American actress

There are no good girls gone wrong, just bad girls found out.
Mae West

Funny really. When you look at the things that go on these days my story reads like Noddy.
Diana Dors (1931-1984), English actress

I am as pure as the driven slush.
Tallulah Bankhead

My literary reputation – or rather lack of it – is
the work of male reviewers who fear female
sexuality and don't like successful women.
Erica Jong

The worst lay in the world. She was always drunk
and she was always eating.
Peter Lawford, actor, on Rita Hayworth

Who cares? I've got the cleanest image in the
world: it's good if there is a little dirt on me.
Cindy Crawford, model, responding to gossip and
media interest about her sexuality and that of husband
Richard Gere

I am a well-known actress. If I wanted to do this
sort of thing, do you really think I'd choose the
A1? If I was that stupid I'd be a policeman.
Gillian Taylforth, English *EastEnders* actress, accused
with her husband of sexual malpractice on an A1 slip-road

I'm just glad I got through my campaign with
most of my life in Britain still classified.
Bill Clinton, on the Home Office's search for files on his
time at Oxford while he was running for President

It's the good girls who keep the diaries; the bad
girls never have the time.
Tallulah Bankhead (1902-1968), American actress

I believe that it's better to be looked over than it is
to be overlooked. And that a girl who keeps her
eyes open is always the kind to look out for.
Mae West (1893-1980)

I know the difference between a good man and
bad one, but I haven't decided which I like better.
Mae West (1893-1980)

RESIGNATION

You have been a most effective minister and I am sorry that your talents will not now be available to the Government.
John Major, MP, in response to Tim Yeo's resignation after revelations of his marital infidelity

When I should so much have liked to be seen as a tower of strength, I am perceived by some as a point of weakness.
David Mellor, MP, in his resignation letter to John Major

Resignations are coming in threes – rather like packets of Mates.
Tony Banks, Labour MP, on the resignation of Michael Mates over the Asil Nadir affair

He has been a fool. I don't know why he had to resign over this. Everyone flirts, don't they?
Local Conservative Party chairman, speaking of Hartley Booth, MP's decision to resign after revelations of his relationship with a researcher at the House of Commons

I suppose it means I'll be having a nine-month leaving party.
James Naughtie, presenter of *World at One*, who was offered a post at Radio 4 in July 1994 to start April 1995

Why don't you resign, you plonker?
Terry Lewis, Labour MP, after the Whips announced Government defeat over the social chapter, House of Commons

RETIREMENT

I married him for better or worse, but not for lunch.
Hazel Weiss, after her husband, George Weiss, retired as general manager of the *New York Yankees*, 1960

Retirement at 65 is ridiculous.
When I was 65, I still had pimples.
George Burns

. . . one sure way of shortening life.
Frank Conklin

Lord Tyrawley and I have been dead these two years, but we don't choose to have it known.
Lord Chesterfield (1694-1773), English statesman

Eating's going to be a whole new ball game. I may even have to buy a new pair of trousers.
Lester Piggot, British champion jockey, on his retirement

Americans hardly ever retire from business; they are either carried out feet first or they jump from a window.
Professor A. L. Goodhart (1891-1978), American lawyer

Few men of action have been able to make a graceful exit at the appropriate time.
Malcolm Muggeridge, British journalist

Retirement is the ugliest word in the language.
Ernest Hemingway (1899-1961)

REVENGE

It's far easier to forgive an enemy after you've got even with him.
Olin Miller, writer

You slap my cheek and I'll turn it. But you slap my wife or my children, boy, and *I'll put you on the floor!*
Dr James Robison, American TV religious personality

Nothing is more costly, nothing is more sterile, than vengeance.
Sir Winston Churchill

ROCK AND ROLL

Wearing very tight striped pants, he looked like a bifurcated marrow . . . like a pensionable cherub.
Clive James, on Rod Stewart

Rock'n'roll is part of a pest to undermine the morals of the youth of our nation. It is sexualistic, unmoralistic and . . . brings people of both races together.
North Alabama White Citizens Council, 1950s

Purgative of all frustrations. It's like going to Confession when I was 10 years old. The weight of wanking would lift from my brain as I told the priest I'd masturbated X times. At gigs, it's the same thing.
Bob Geldof, singer

Rock and roll is about cocks and jiving and the odd bloody nose . . . and about people like us talking seriously about the social order.
Jean-Jacques Burnel, bass guitarist with *The Stranglers*

Zimmer Rock Rules – Peace, love and a comforting cup of ovaltine.
Phil Norman, biographer of the Beatles and Rolling Stones, referring to a number of the rock stars of the sixties who are still going strong

The British Rock and Pop Awards – So inconsequential that it wasn't even offensive, it had the lasting importance of someone breaking wind in the middle of a hurricane.
Clive James

Rock'n'Roll is the most brutal, ugly, vicious form of expression it has been my misfortune to hear – sly, lewd, in plan fact, dirty. It manages to be the martial music of every sideburned delinquent on the face of the earth. This rancid smelling aphrodisiac I deplore.
Frank Sinatra

Rock'n'Roll is instant coffee.
Bob Geldof, singer

His triumphs in singles like *It's not Unusual* and *Delilah* have earned him a permanent niche in the annuals of nursing-home rock.
John Swenson, on singer Tom Jones

If Rock'n'Roll is here to stay I might commit suicide.
Sammy Davis Jr.

The Rolling Stones . . .

He's stoned on himself. He's always in complete control and the whole thing is manipulation. It really bothers me that a twerp like that can parade around and convince everybody that he's Satan.
Ry Cooder, on Mick Jagger

Mick Jagger has big lips. He can play a tuba from both ends. This man has got child-bearing lips . . .
Joan Rivers

Nine months of listening to the Rolling Stones is not my idea of heaven.
Mick Jagger, after completing the record *Love You Live*, 1977

If the Stones' lyrics made sense, they wouldn't be any good.
Truman Capote (attrib.)

He moves like a parody between a majorette girl and Fred Astaire.
Truman Capote of Mick Jagger (attrib.)

They look like boys whom any self-respecting mum would lock in the bathroom.
The Daily Express, 1964

SCANDALS

There is something utterly nauseating about a system of society which pays a harlot 25 times as much as it pays its Prime Minister, 250 times as much as it pays its Members of Parliament, and 500 times as much as it pays some of its ministers of religion.
Harold Wilson, British Prime Minister, referring to the Christine Keeler case in a House of Commons speech, June 1963

A great party is not to be brought down because of a scandal by a woman of easy virtue and a proved liar.
Lord Hailsham, British Conservative politician, referring to the Profumo affair, on a *BBC* interview, June 1963

Love and scandal are the best sweeteners of tea.
Henry Fielding (1707-1754), *Love in Several Masques*

One should never make one's debut with a
scandal. One should reserve that to give an interest
to one's old age.
Oscar Wilde, *The Picture of Dorian Gray,* 1891

A stink is still worse for the stirring.
Miguel de Cervantes (1547-1616)

History is made in the class struggle and not in
bed.
Alex Mitchell, British left-wing journalist following the
deposition of the leader of the Worker's Revolutionary
Party, amid a sex scandal, 1985

It is a public scandal that gives offence, and it is
no sin to sin in secret.
Molière, *Tartuffe*

John Major says his cabinet is one big happy
family. Not like that of the Earl of Caithness,
David Mellor and Tim Yeo one hopes.
Stuart Leather, journalist, referring to recent scandals
involving members of parliament

I said it was better to have two parents than one.
That is quite obviously true.
John Redwood, Welsh Secretary, on minister Tim Yeo,
whose former mistress had his child

It occurs to me that there is a simple and practical
method of putting this long-suffering government
out of its misery. My proposition is this: since sex
scandals appear to be the only method of
dislodging a minister – or indeed, any other
politician – from his post it is now the duty of
every patriotic woman in Britain to bear a love
child by a Tory MP.
Margarette Driscoll, writer, *The Sunday Times,* 1994

The scandal has stayed in the public memory
because it had a classic plot, a romantic beginning
and a tragic ending.
The Scotsman, referring to the Profumo affair, 1993

Caesar's wife must be above suspicion.
Julius Caesar (100-44BC), said in justification of his
divorce from Pompeia, after she was unwittingly involved
in a scandal

SCHOOL

O vain futile frivolous boy. Smirking. I won't have
it. I won't have it. I won't have it. Go find the
headmaster and ask him to beat you within an
inch of your life. And say please.
Alan Bennett, Forty Years On, 1968

Show me the man who has enjoyed his schooldays
and I will show you a bully and a bore.
Robert Morley, Robert Morley: Responsible Gentleman,
1966

My school motto was 'Monsanto incorpori glorius
maxima copia' which in Latin means, 'When the
going gets tough the tough go shopping'.
Robin Williams

Stand firm in your refusal to remain conscious
during algebra. In real life, I assure you, there is no
such thing as algebra.
Fran Lebowitz, Social Studies, 1981

SEDUCTION

The difference between rape and ecstasy is
salesmanship.
Lord Thomson of Fleet (1894-1976), Canadian
publisher

The resistance of a woman is not always proof of
her virtue, but more often of her experience.
Ninon de Lenclos (1620-1705), French society lady and
wit

Sensuality and eroticism are tools that I decide
consciously to use.
Kathleen Turner, American actress

I was seduced . . . in the sense that I had an affair
with her. I did not have sex with her.
Hartley Booth, MP, admitting to an affair with his
Commons research assistant, 1994

By keeping men off, you keep them on.
John Gay (1685-1732), English playwright

If men knew all that women think, they'd be 20
times more daring.
Alphonse Karr (1808-1890), French novelist and
journalist

Men who do not make advances to women are apt
to become victims to women who make advances
to them.
Walter Bagehot (1826-1877), English economist and
journalist

She has the mouth of Marilyn Monroe, and the
eyes of Caligula.
Francois Mitterrand, of Margaret Thatcher

Older women are best because they always think
they may be doing it for the last time.
Ian Fleming (1908-1964), British author

The trouble with Ian is that he gets off with
women because he can't get on with them.
Rosamund Lehmann, British author, of Ian Fleming

To succeed with the opposite sex, tell her you're
impotent. She can't wait to disprove it.
Cary Grant (1904-1986)

A woman will sometimes forgive the man who
tries to seduce her, but never the man who misses
an opportunity when offered.
Charles-Maurice de Talleyrand (1754-1838), French
bishop and politician

I tried to charm the pants off Bob Dylan but
everyone will be disappointed to learn that I was
unsuccessful. I got close . . . a couple of fast feels
in the front seat of his Cadillac.
Bette Midler, American film star, *Rolling Stone,* 1982

The mind can also be an erogenous zone.
Raquel Welch

SEX

I don't think sex has much to do with morals. It's more a compulsion – like murder.
Alice Thomas Ellis, writer

Continental people have a sex life; the English have hot-water bottles.
George Mikes, *How to be an Alien*

Sex is meant for procreation, and I want to consummate a relationship with a man who's going to be the father of my children.
Brooke Shields, American actress

I'm suggesting we call sex something else, and it should include everything from kissing to sitting close together.
Shere Hite, American writer

I know we're in the sexual spotlight at the moment, but sex is always high on the political agenda. I was selected for Billericay after the peccadilloes of my predecessor, Harvey Proctor, caused a scandal.
Teresa Gorman, MP

Her memoirs are so depressing; she's had so few men. It seems she's never had a happy day – or night – in her life.
Joan Crawford, on Bette Davis

I've had sex in a car with everything except a giraffe.
Larry Adler, musician

Laughter can be an aphrodisiac, yet it can also be a substitute for sex.
Zoe Wanamaker, British actress

My brain: it's my second favourite organ.
Woody Allen, Sleeper

Great sex always makes you laugh.
Kathleen Turner, American actress

I've got more sex in my little finger than she has in her whole body, and I'm out to prove it.
Kim Basinger, American film star, of Madonna

Sex is emotion in motion
Mae West

The only reason I would take up jogging is so I could hear heavy breathing again.
Erma Bombeck

I know nothing about sex, because I was always married.
Zsa Zsa Gabor

Maybe I'm not talented. Maybe I'm just the Dinah Shore of the sixties. The square people think I'm too hip and the hip people think I'm too square. And nobody likes my choice of men. Everybody thinks I'm fucking the Mormon Tabernacle Choir.
Cher, American actress and singer

I don't see much of Alfred any more since he got so interested in sex.
Mrs Alfred Kinsey, wife of the author of the *Kinsey Report on Sexual Behaviour*

Love is the answer, but while you're waiting for the answer, sex raises some pretty good questions.
Woody Allen

You remember your first mountain in much the same way you remember having your first sexual experience, except that climbing doesn't make as much mess and you don't cry for a week if Ben Nevis forgets to phone next morning.
Muriel Gray, TV presenter and writer, *The First Fifty,* 1990

I think I made his back feel better.
Marilyn Monroe, after a private meeting with John F. Kennedy

I get very sexually excited on stage. It's like making love to 9,000 people at once.
Prince, rock musician

I'd rather have a nice cup of tea.
Boy George, musician

There are a lot more interesting things in life than sex – like reading.
Jean Alexander, the actress who played Hilda Ogden in ITV's *Coronation Street*

Boats, cars, sex . . . you have to touch all of them lightly or they lose their glamour.
Mel Gibson, Australian actor

It's the most fun I ever had without laughing.
Woody Allen

Sex is good for you. I'd rather die making love than in any other way.
Edward Woodward, British actor

I can't help it, I've been this way since I was five.
Rob Lowe, American actor, after spending time in a clinic to cure an apparent addiction to sex

I don't know anyone who laughs *during* orgasm. Sex is serious. On the other hand, I'm not saying *foreplay* is.
Raquel Welch

Sex has to be behind locked doors. If what you're doing can be done out in the open, you may as well be pitching horseshoes.
George Burns

I don't care about sex any more. Its been years since I made love. Nowadays I so much prefer motorcycles.
Mickey Rourke

I don't say anything during sex. I've been told not to. Told during sex, in fact.
Chevy Chase

Sex for a fat man is much a do about puffing.
Jackie Gleason

It's not all that important to me. It would be important if I wasn't getting any.
Michael Caine

I'm preoccupied by sex – an area of human behaviour that's underexplored in general. And I like virgin territory.
Jack Nicholson

It's best natural.
Robert Redford

People have always found my sex life of interest, but I can do without sex.
Pamela Bordes, call-girl turned photographer

They say sex is as good as a five mile run. I don't think I move five miles making love, but we've got three bedrooms. Make of that what you will.
Michael Palin, British actor

Good sex is absolutely wonderful for you – much better than jogging.
Jilly Cooper, novelist

When two people make love, there are at least four people present – the two, who are actually there and the two they are thinking about.
Sigmund Freud

Sex in a love relationship is always better. I know a lot more about sex now – there's no more of that frantic fumbling and groping that went on when you were young.
Paul Daniels, British magician

I know it does make people happy but to me it is just like having a cup of tea.
Cynthia Payne, after her acquittal over the famous sex for lunch vouchers case, 1987

It was just one of those things which, if you had been to bed before marriage, you would presumably have known.
Barbara Cartland

Watch sex. It is the key to success and the trap door to failure.
Michael Shea, director of Public Affairs, Hanson Plc

Last time I tried to make love to my wife nothing was happening, so I said to her what's the matter, you can't think of anybody either?
Rodney Dangerfield

Sex is the biggest nothing of all time.
Andy Warhol

Are you going to come quietly or do I have to use earplugs?
The Goon Show

Ducking for apples – change one letter and it's the story of my life.
Dorothy Parker

Some men are all right in their place – if they only knew the right places.
Mae West

I've tried several varieties of sex. The conventional position makes me claustrophobic. And the others either give me a stiff neck or lockjaw.
Tallulah Bankhead

My husband is German; every night I get dressed up like Poland and he invades me.
Bette Midler

The important thing in acting is to be able to laugh and cry. If I have to cry, I think of my sex life. If I have to laugh, I think of my sex life.
Glenda Jackson

I didn't get ahead by sleeping with people. Girls take heart.
Barbara Walters, American television presenter

I've only slept with the men I've been married to. How many women can make that claim?
Elizabeth Taylor

Personally I like sex and I don't care what a man thinks of me as long as I get what I want from him – which is usually sex.
Valerie Perrine, American film actress

I've never taken up with a congressman in my life . . . I've never gone below the Senate.
Barbara Howar

It has to be admitted that we English have sex on the brain which is a very unsatisfactory place to have it.
Malcolm Muggeridge, British journalist

Sex is a pleasurable exercise in plumbing, but be careful or you'll get yeast in your drain pipe.
Rita Mae Brown

Sex is like having dinner, sometimes you joke about the dishes, sometimes you take the meal seriously.
Woody Allen

And remember, there's nothing these women won't do to satisfy
Their ever-moist groins; they've just one obsession – sex.
Juvenal (60-140AD), Roman satirist and poet, *Satires X*

When a man and woman of unorthodox tastes make love, the man could be said to be introducing his foible into her quirk.
Kenneth Tynan, English theatre critic

Being bald is an unfailing sex magnet.
Telly Savalas, actor

It's a flesh market; you won't find finer flesh anywhere.
Julia Morley, British organiser, Miss World

Well built without being the slightest bit sexy, like a junior minister's wife.
Denis Norden, describing a certain woman's lack of sex appeal

I've spent time with her and she's everything a man could want. She's a very warm, beautiful, intelligent and sexy lady.
Sylvester Stallone, of Fergie, the Duchess of York

You don't have to hit anybody on the head with four letter words to be sexy.
Eartha Kitt, singer

I am the world's sexiest man.
Noel Coward (1899-1973)

Fat people are brilliant in bed. If I'm sitting on top of you, who's going to argue?
Jo Brand, comedienne

Sex, treated properly, can be one of the most gorgeous things in the world.
Elizabeth Taylor

Windows last longer than sex, whatever way you look at it.
The Duchess of Devonshire, urging more architectural and fewer sex lessons in schools

Big women are sexier than thin ones – we pump more oestrogen, have higher sex drives and fantasise more. Men love big girls in a sort of closet way, but often don't like to be seen out with them. Being big is a sign of fertility, of voluptuous sensuality, a love of life. That's a very inviting thing.
Dawn French

The nearest I've been to a sexual experience lately is finding lipstick on a cafe cup.
Guy Bellamy, The Secret Lemonade Drinker

He worked out that I would have ten thousand bonks during my life and said it was really selfish of me not to give him a bonk for £10K.

Young clerk speaking at an industrial tribunal about her boss

Sex without using someone is as difficult as eating without chewing.

Julie Burchill, writer and journalist, *Observer*, 1986

I'm tired, send one of them home.

Mae West, on being told that ten men were waiting to meet her

You know, the worst thing about oral sex? The view.

Maureen Lipman, British writer and actress

SEX AIDS

There are a number of mechanical devices which increase sexual arousal, particularly in women. Chief among these is the Mercedes-Benz 380SL convertible.

P. J. O'Rourke

Det. Inspector Roy Penrose said in a statement read to the court that a booklet advertising artificial male organs was found by police at Miss Jones's home in May.

They also found a vibrating device hidden inside a pouffé.

The hearing continues today.

The Birmingham Post, quoted in *Private Eye*

SEX APPEAL

If a man doesn't look at me when I walk into a room, he's gay.

Kathleen Turner

We need heroes. Whether or not it pleases you, Mr Connery, we have decided that you will be our hero.

Princess Anne, at a film premiere, to Sean Connery

I'm more the thinking woman's crumbling ruin. I always wear the same suit on the programme so people don't notice me.
Melvyn Bragg, host, *South Bank Show*

I have had propositions, but I don't take them up. The family can't understand how anyone can fancy me. But then, neither can I.
Barry Norman, film critic

I'm in my seventies. What could she possibly see in me – is she into necrophilia or something?
Dirk Bogarde, British actor and novelist, on a request by Madonna to include him in her book *Sex*

Plunging necklines attract more attention and cost less money.
Shelley Winters, American actress

She sounded like the Book of Revelations read out over a railway station public address system by a headmistress of a certain age, wearing calico knickers.
Clive James, describing Margaret Thatcher on television

If Canada is underdeveloped so is Brigitte Bardot.
H. R. Macmillan

Being a sex symbol is a heavy load to carry, especially when one is tired, hurt and bewildered.
Clara Bow (1905-1965), US film actress

You can't be a movie star without it – and it's a big burden.
Jane Fonda

One can act sexuality to a certain extent. But there's a grey area there. Nobody can be petted, touched and kissed without feeling something. 'Cut!' is a very good cold shower!
Kathleen Turner

Where do you think I'd be if I hadn't got whistles?
Marilyn Monroe

Sex appeal is in your heart and head. I'd be sexy no matter how old or how my body changes.
Sonia Braga

SEX TIPS

Another tip: If you were planning to have an affair, it would be better to lay off lay preachers. Now, if you want to be a research assistant at Westminster, you must decide which party you want to support and never give a quote to anybody on the subject of orgasms, condoms, etc. It will only ever be used against you and your Member.
Julia Langdon, British journalist

Since Mozart's day composers have learned the art of making music throatily and palpitatingly sexual.
Aldous Huxley (1894-1964), *Along the Road*, of popular music

Everyone has a duty to use their natural assets, be it beauty, brains or brawn.
Jerry Hall, American model

I like playing the field. Life can get rather exciting when lots of men are calling you, each of them offering a different activity.
Brooke Shields, actress

SEXUAL ATTRACTION

There's a side to being in England and being with Englishmen that seems to bring out the devil in me.
Debra Winger, American actress

If De Niro puts on weight, he's a great actor. If a woman does it, she's getting old and out of shape. I've learnt that now.
Kathleen Turner, American actress, talking about keeping fit

Capable motherly types adore him. One look at the crumpled shirt, the tie askew and the flyaway hair is enough to arouse a deep-seated maternal instinct. Even power-suited girls who wouldn't be seen dead ironing their lover's shirts long to sort out John's curling collars. Grandmothers yearn to do up his top button and smile when he tucks his shirt tails into his Y-fronts.
Lynn Barber, referring to Prime Minister Major's appeal to women

That's it baby, if you've got it, flaunt it.
Mel Brooks, US film actor and director, *The Producers*

A beauty is a woman you notice; a charmer is one who notices you.
Adlai Stevenson, American politician and lawyer

A woman may develop wrinkles and cellulite, lose her waistline, her bustline, her ability to bear a child, even her sense of humour, but none of that implies a loss of sexuality, her femininity.
Barbara Gordon, American TV producer and writer

Sex Appeal Swung Him Into Oval Office . . .
A *Today* analysis of Bill Clinton's victory shows a combination of caring policies, sex and power helped him win. Victorious Bill Clinton hailed the women of America after their massive support put him in the White House. About 60 per cent ignored accusations of womanising and voted for him.
Today, 1993

Being a sex symbol has to do with an attitude, not looks. Most men think it's looks, most women know otherwise.
Kathleen Turner, American actress

Her body is arranged the way it is, to display it to the man looking at the picture. The picture is made to appeal to *his* sexuality. It has nothing to do with her sexuality . . . Women are there to feed an appetite, not to have any of their own.
John Berger, British writer, describing the construction of advertising images, *Ways of Seeing,* 1972

What's so fucking wrong with being a sex symbol?
Kris Kristofferson, American singer and actor

If people think I'm a dumb blonde because of the way I look, then they're dumber than they think I am. If people think I'm not very deep because of my wigs and outfits, then they're not very deep.
Dolly Parton, US singer and songwriter

The lady may never have been for turning but she certainly turned heads. Everybody flirted with the Prime Minister. I think she took it as her due that you should flirt with her.
Alan Clark, former defence minister, referring to Margaret Thatcher

Many a man in love with a dimple makes the mistake of marrying the wrong girl.
Stephen Leacock, English-born Canadian economist and humorist, *Literary Lapses,* 1910

Being a sex symbol is rather like being a convict.
Raquel Welch, American actress

She is Hollywood's fantasy infanta, its damsel in shining armour, its good girl scout. Poised eternally between childhood and womanhood, she is sexy but not sexual – and as threatening as a piece of angel cake.
Graham Fuller, executive editor of *Interview Magazine,* of Julia Roberts, film star

Sex appeal is 50 per cent what you've got and 50 per cent what people think you've got.
Sophia Loren, Italian actress

One girl can be pretty – but a dozen are only a chorus.
F. Scott Fitzgerald (1896-1940), US novelist, *The Last Tycoon,* 1941

What, when drunk, one sees in other women, one sees in Garbo sober.
Kenneth Tynan (1927-1980), British theatre critic

God, I think after dark probably I draw them more.
Britt Ekland, when asked what draws men to her

A lot of women are frightened of losing their looks, jobs, husband, children or reputation. I wouldn't be fazed by any of these.
Britt Ekland

Sex appeal is not about how you look, it's about energy and inner strength. I've dated all sorts: fat ones, skinny ones, black, white Japanese, everything. It does not matter how you look.
Denyce Graves, American mezzo-soprano

Actors like him are good but on the whole I do not enjoy actors who seek to commune with their armpits, so to speak.
Greer Garson, of actor Marlon Brando

J. M. Barrie's Tinkerbell was all brains and no body, whereas Julia Roberts . . .
Jill Parkin, of Julia Roberts, actress who played Tinkerbell, in the film *Hook*

I think Mick Jagger would be astounded and amazed if he realized to how many people he is not a sex symbol.
Angie Bowie, ex-wife of David Bowie

I'm Number 10 at the box office. Right under Barbra Streisand. Can you imagine being under Barbra Streisand? Give me a bag.
I may throw up.
Walter Matthau, American actor

A man with the sex appeal of a sheep and the comic timing of a manatee.
Chris Peachment, journalist and critic, of Richard Chamberlain

Co-star Helen Mirren continues her determined bid to give up acting for the role of ripest screen-tease object of the 80s.
Rod McShane, journalist and critic

The idea of two Van Dammes must have seemed workable on paper . . . but both exude the charisma of a packet of Cup-A-Soup.
Jonathan Romney, journalist and critic, on actor Jean-Claude Van Damme's performance in *Double Impact*

They labelled me the 'Ooomph Girl'. To me,
'Ooomph' is the sound that a fat man makes when
he bends over to tie his shoelaces in a phone
booth.
Ann Sheridan, actress

SHAME

Shame is the feeling you have when you agree with
the woman who loves you that you are the man
she thinks you are.
Carl Sandburg (1878-1967), American poet

Whoever blushes is already guilty; true innocence
is not ashamed of anything.
Jean-Jacques Rousseau (1712-1778)

SHOPPING

Sex, pure and simple, is about shopping. Some
people shop at Harrods, some at Marks &
Spencer.
If it's love that you want, tenderness, a mutual
exchange of hope, despair, fear, then this isn't the
market for you.
Lindi St Clair, prostitute

Years ago a person, he was unhappy, didn't know
what to do with himself – he'd go to church, start
a revolution – *something.* Today you're unhappy?
Can't figure it out? What is the salvation? Go
shopping.
Arthur Miller, US dramatist, *The Price*

Money dignifies what is frivolous if unpaid for.
Virginia Woolf (1882-1941)

S I N

Sin is a dangerous toy in the hands of the virtuous. It should be left to the congenitally sinful, who know when to play with it and when to let it alone.
H. L. Mencken, *The American Mercury,* 1929

Pleasure is something that you feel that you should really enjoy, which is really virtuous, but you don't; and sin's something that you're quite sure you shouldn't enjoy but do.
Ralph Wightman, radio presenter

A sin tends to be addictive, and the terminal of addiction is what is called damnation.
W. H. Auden (1907-1973), British poet, *A Certain World*

Shoot all the bluejays you want. If you can't, hit 'em, but remember it's a sin to kill a mockingbird.
Harper Lee, US writer, *To Kill a Mockingbird*

Few love to hear the sins they love to act.
William Shakespeare, *Pericles*

Should we all confess our sins to one another we would all laugh at one another for our lack or originality.
Kahil Gibran (1883-1931), Syrian mystic and poet

A private sin is not so prejudicial in the world as a public indecency.
Miguel de Cervantes (1577-1616), Spanish novelist

That which we call sin in others, is experiment for us.
R. W. Emerson (1803-1882), American essayist, poet and philosopher

Commit a sin twice and it will not seem a crime.
Rabbinical saying

Fashions in sin change.
Lillian Hellman, *Watch on the Rhine,* 1941

Many are saved from sin by being so inept at it.
Mignon McLaughlin, American author

For God's sake, if you sin, take pleasure in it,
And do it for the pleasure . . .
Gerald Gould (1885-1936), British poet

Nothing makes one so vain as being told that one
is a sinner.
Oscar Wilde

THE SIXTIES

All that Swinging Sixties nonsense, we all thought
it was passé at the time.
David Bailey, British photographer

I was appalled when the San Francisco ethic didn't
mushroom and envelop the whole world into this
loving community of acid freaks. I was very naïve.
Grace Slick, American rock singer

They'd go up to a table and tell people, 'Hello, I'm
your waitress. How's your energy today? Our
lunch special is the Gestalt Suchi – we give you a
live fish, and you take the responsibility for killing
it.'
Robin Williams, 1982

SLANDER

I will make a bargain with the Democrats. If they
will stop telling lies about Republicans we will
stop telling the truth about them.
Chauncey Depew (1834-1928), American Republican
politician

Lie lustily, some filth will stick.
Thomas Hall (1610-1665), English preacher and author

It is perfectly monstrous the way people go about
nowadays saying things against one, behind one's
back, that are absolutely and entirely true.
Oscar Wilde

S M E L L S

The woman one loves always smells good.
Remy de Gourmont (1858-1915), French critic and
novelist

I did not realise what it had done to my breath –
one doesn't with garlic – until this afternoon when
I stood waiting for somebody to open a door for
me and suddenly noticed that the varnish on the
door was bubbling.
Frank Muir, *You Can't Have your Kayak and Heat It,*
1973

I counted two and seventy stenches,
All well defined, and several stinks!
S. T. Coleridge (1772-1834), of Cologne

Of nothing are you allowed to get the real odour
or savour. Everything is sterilised and wrapped in
cellophane. The only odour which is recognised
and admitted as an odour is halitosis and of this
all Americans live in mortal dread.
Henry Miller (1891-1980)

S M O K I N G

Smoking is a dying habit.
Virginia Bottomley, health secretary

I never smoked a cigarette until I was nine.
W. C. Fields (attrib.)

A custom loathsome to the eye, hateful to the
nose, harmful to the brain, dangerous to the lungs,
and in the black, stinking fume thereof nearest
resembling the horrible Stygian smoke of the pit
that is bottomless.
King James VI and I (1566-1625)

There's nothing quite like tobacco; it's the passion
of decent folk, and whoever lives without tobacco
doesn't deserve to live.
Molière (1622-1673)

A cigarette is the perfect type of a perfect pleasure.
It is exquisite and it leaves one unsatisfied.
Oscar Wilde

I needed a vice real quick.
Mia Farrow, American actress, confessing that she only
started to smoke during relationship problems with Woody
Allen

Smoking is, if not my life, then at least my hobby.
I love to smoke. Smoking is fun. Smoking is cool.
Smoking is, as far as I am concerned, the entire
point of being an adult.
Fran Lebowitz, Social Studies, 1981

Sometimes a cigar is just a cigar.
Sigmund Freud, on being asked by a student whether
his cigar smoking was a symbolic activity

I thought I couldn't afford to take her out and
smoke as well. So I gave up cigarettes. Then I took
her out and one day I looked at her and thought,
oh well, and I went back to smoking again, and
that was better.
Benny Hill, on a girlfriend he had when earning 27s 6d a
week

Smokers, male and female, inject and excuse
idleness in their lives every time they light a
cigarette.
Colette

But when I don't smoke I scarcely feel as if I'm
living. I don't feel as if I'm living unless I'm killing
myself.
Russell Hoban, British author

For thy sake, Tobacco, I would do anything but
die.
Charles Lamb (1775-1834), English writer

I kissed my first woman and smoked my first
cigarette on the same day; I have never had time
for tobacco since.
Arturo Toscanini (1867-1957), Italian conductor

Lighten up Al. Take a breath, inhale.
Dan Quayle, Vice President of USA, remark made in reference to Al Gore, Democratic vice-presidential nominee, to Bill Clinton's admission that he smoked pot at Oxford but didn't inhale

And a woman is only a woman, but a good cigar is a smoke.
Rudyard Kipling (1865-1936), Indian-born British writer and poet

I have every sympathy with the American who was so horrified by what he had read of the effects of smoking that he gave up reading.
Henry G. Strauss (later Lord Conesford), politician

I'm that age now where just putting my cigar in its holder is a thrill.
George Burns

I guess President Clinton and I will not be able to smoke our peace pipes in the White House.
Fidel Castro, on a smoking ban imposed by Hillary Clinton

SNOBBERY

She [his aunt] was a bit of a social climber – although very much on the lower slopes. I was once on a tram with her going past the gas works in Wellington Road and she said, 'Alan, this is the biggest gas works in England. And I know the manager.'
Alan Bennett, British playwright

Snobbery – the 'pox Britannica'.
Anthony Sampson, British journalist and author

Snobs talk as if they had begotten their own ancestors.
Herbert Agar (1897-1980), American author and journalist

Laughter would be bereaved if snobbery died.
Peter Ustinov, British actor and wit

Philistine – a term of contempt applied by prigs to the rest of their species.
Sir Leslie Stephen (1832-1904), British author and philosopher

Respectable means rich, and decent means poor. I should die if I heard my family called decent.
Thomas Love Peacock (1785-1866), English author

S P E E C H E S

The most difficult things for a man to do are to climb a wall leaning towards you, to kiss a girl leaning away from you, and to make an after-dinner speech.
Winston Churchill

An after-dinner speech should be like a lady's dress – long enough to cover the subject and short enough to be interesting.
R. A. Butler

Spontaneous speeches are seldom worth the paper they are written on.
Leslie Henson, The Observer, 1943

When a man gets up to speak, people listen, then look. When a woman gets up, people look, then if they like what they see, they listen.
Pauline Frederick, American news correspondent

The human brain starts working the moment you are born and never stops until you stand up to speak in public.
Sir George Jessel, Solicitor-General and Master of the Rolls

A speech is like a love affair. Any fool can start it, but to end it requires considerable skill.
Lord Mancroft

It usually takes me more than three weeks to prepare a good impromptu speech.
Mark Twain

SPORT

Serious sport has nothing to do with fair play. It is bound up with hatred, jealousy, boastfullness, disregard of all rules and sadistic pleasure in witnessing violence: in other words it is war minus the shooting.
George Orwell, The Sporting Spirit, 1945

They thought lacrosse was what you find at la church.
Robin Williams

STARDOM

Being a star has made it possible for me to get insulted in places where the average Negro could never hope to get insulted.
Sammy Davis Jr.

There is not a more unhappy being than a superannuated idol.
Joseph Addison (1672-1719), English essayist

In America I had two secretaries – one for autographs and the other for locks of hair. Within six months one had died of writer's cramp, and the other was completely bald.
Oscar Wilde

STYLE

Atilla the Hen.
Clement Freud, of Margaret Thatcher

She cannot see an institution without hitting it with her handbag.
Julian Critchley, of Margaret Thatcher

Style is knowing who you are, what you want to say, and not giving a damn.
Gore Vidal

In the '80s I led the life of Riley. Unfortunately it was Mavis Riley from Coronation Street. It was s***.
Jo Brand, comedienne

Style is self plagiarism.
Alfred Hitchcock

No style is good that is not fit to be spoken or read aloud with effect.
William Hazlitt (1778-1830)

I hate lines under my jeans.
Bruce Springsteen, American singer, to Los Angeles shop staff, when buying Speedo G-strings

I live in the moment. The '70s, the '80s even, are like 1,000 years ago.
Calvin Klein, designer

Glamour is what makes a man ask for your telephone number. But it also is what makes a woman ask for the name of your dressmaker.
Lilly Dache, French-born US fashion designer and writer

There is no such thing as a moral dress . . . It's people who are moral or immoral.
Jennie Jerome Churchill (1854-1921), British hostess, editor and playwright

Her frocks are built in Paris but she wears them with a strong English accent.
Saki, Reginald on Women, 1895

If I'm too strong for some people, that's their problem.
Glenda Jackson, English actress and MP

Luck is a matter of preparation meeting opportunity.
Oprah Winfrey, American talk show host and actress

SUCCESS

I'm the luckiest bitch on the face of the planet. It's that simple.
Whoopi Goldberg, US film star, on her success

Success is like champagne – everyone should have some.
Zoe Wanamaker, British actress

I am the American dream.
Diana Ross, American singer

Powerful men often succeed through the help of their wives. Powerful women only succeed in spite of their husbands.
Linda Lee-Potter, British journalist, 1984

TABOO

To make our idea of morality centre on forbidden acts is to defile the imagination and to introduce into our judgments of our fellow-men a secret element of gusto.
Robert Louis Stevenson (1850-1894)

Perhaps the long ages during which pork had been prohibited had made it seem to the Jews as delicious as fornication.
Bertrand Russell

In a non-permissive age, she made remarkable inroads against the taboos of her day, and did so without even lowering her neckline.
Leslie Halliwell, British journalist and author, of Mae West

TAXATION

All money nowadays seems to be produced with a natural homing instinct for the Treasury.
Duke of Edinburgh

Taxes cause crime. When the tax rate reaches 25 per cent, there is an increase in lawlessness. America's tax system is inspired by Karl Marx.
Ronald Reagan

The avoidance of taxes is the only pursuit that still carries any reward.
John Maynard Keynes (1883-1946)

To produce an income tax return that has any depth to it, any feeling, one must have Lived and Suffered.
Frank Sullivan (1892-1976), American humorist and journalist

We are looking for a wealth tax that will bring in sufficient revenue to justify having a wealth tax.
Dick Spring, leader of the Irish Labour Party

Read my lips: No new taxes.
George Bush, his promise made during the 1988 Presidential campaign

The income tax has made more liars out of the American people than golf has. Even when you make a tax form out on the level, you don't know when it's through if you are a crook or a martyr.
Will Rogers

Blessed are the young, for they shall inherit the national debt.
D. Herbert Hoover

TECHNOLOGY

The drive towards complex technical achievement offers a clue to why the US is good at space gadgetry and bad at slum problems.
J. K. Galbraith, American economist

Any sufficiently advanced technology is indistinguishable from magic.
Arthur C. Clarke, British author

One machine can do the work of fifty ordinary men. No machine can do the work of one extraordinary man.
Elbert Hubbard

TELEVISION

Television is a whore. Any man who wants her full favours can have them in five minutes with a pistol.
Anon

Television has something in common with the world of racing: it is crowded with untrustworthy characters and bristles with opportunities to cheat.
Paul Johnson, British journalist

I find television very educational. Every time someone switches it on I go into another room and read a good book.
Groucho Marx (1890-1977)

I hate television. I hate it as much as peanuts. But I can't stop eating peanuts.
Orson Welles (1915-1985)

Let's face it, there are no plain women on television.
Anna Ford, British television personality

Television is an invention that permits you to be entertained in your living room by people you wouldn't have in your home.
Sir David Frost, British television personality

I made a remark a long time ago. I said I was very pleased that television was now showing murder stories, because it's bringing murder back into its rightful setting – in the home.
Alfred Hitchcock (1889-1980), British film director

Television is the kind of thing you pay attention to if you wish, and if you don't you go to clean out your drawers.
Cher

Good heavens, television is something you appear on, you don't watch it.
Noel Coward

In California, they don't throw their garbage away – they make it into TV shows.
Woody Allen

American television must raise its ceiling by some method other than lowering the floor.
Jack Gould, The New York Times, 1966

In certain situations, when things are emotionally intense – if there is conflict, for instance – I still can't speak. I can't start, or more often, finish my sentences.
Gerard Depardieu, French actor, on why he doesn't take part in television chat shows

Children watch too much TV not only because indolent parents allow them to, but because the standard of most programmes is pitched at their level.
Richard Ingrams, writer and satirist

Acting on television is like being asked by the captain to entertain the passengers while the ship goes down.
Peter Ustinov

TEMPERANCE

Sobriety's a real turn-on for me. You can see what you're doing.
Peter O'Toole

One reason I don't drink is that I want to know when I'm having a good time.
Nancy Astor

I don't drink. I don't like it. It makes me feel good.
Oscar Levant

I don't drink, because when I drank I used to hit people.
Billy Connolly, Scottish comedian

What a strange paradox it is that I would be unemployable if I were teetotal.
Jeffrey Bernard, British journalist

TEMPTATION

I can resist everything except temptation
Oscar Wilde, *Lady Windermere's Fan,* 1892

Why resist temptation – there will always be more.
Don Herold, American humorist, writer and artist

A little of what you fancy does you good.
Marie Lloyd (1870-1922), British music hall entertainer

. . . there are terrible temptations that it requires strength, strength and courage to yield to.
Oscar Wilde, An Ideal Husband, 1895

Thou strong seducer, Opportunity.
John Dryden (1631-1700)

I am not over-fond of resisting temptation.
William Beckford (1759-1844), English author

Honest bread is very well – it's the butter that makes the temptation.
Douglas Jerrold (1803-1857), English playwright and humorist

There are two things in life I cannot resist – sticky puddings and beautiful women. Why? Because I'm a man and that's what men like.
Richard Branson

A good many young writers make the mistake of enclosing a stamped self-addressed envelope, big enough for the manuscript to come back in. This is too much of a temptation for the editor.
Ring Lardner, How to Write Short Stories

Although the temptations were there, I tended to pull away. Even now, I think, 'What would my mum say if she knew I was here, or saying this or doing that?'
Cliff Richard, British singer, 1993

TENNIS

Could someone please come and check on Kathy Rinaldi's knickers?
Call to Wimbledon headquarters from official monitoring the 'predominantly white' rule

I washed it.
Conchita Martinez, on why her skirt, which had infringed Wimbledon's all white regulations, was allowed two days later

Now he's even more gorgeous. I love the Chippendales because they are really smooth-looking and with his great suntan he's every bit as lovely as them.
Fan commenting on Andre Agassi's body shave

. . . I don't have much body hair either.
Martina Navratilova

Tennis is a chauvinistic sport . . . you are just some lady waiting for her husband to finish his match and go home. I was treated like a bimbo.
Tatum O'Neal, on her mistreatment as Mrs McEnroe

THEATRE

I'm a very mild woman, as my friend sitting next to me will tell you, and I love coming to the Theatre Royal. And I don't know what it was, but when you hit her, I nearly stood up and shouted 'Kill the bitch!'. And I find myself absolutely appalled by what I nearly did.
Member of *Oleanna* audience in Bath

[At the end] we hold on to each other very tightly, to remind ourselves that we actually like each other.
Lia Williams, actress, on David Suchet, her sparring partner in the sex-war play, *Oleanna*

Drama never changed anybody's mind about anything.
David Mamet, author of *Oleanna*

How beautiful, how ridiculous and oh, how infinitely sad.
Evening Standard verdict on the revival of *Hair*

I can't be sacked, you see, because I haven't got a job. Therefore I'll continue to say whatever I like.
Harold Pinter, writer and playwright

T I M E

Procrastination – the art of keeping up with yesterday.
Don Marquis (1878-1937), American writer

The further backward you can look, the further forward you are likely to see.
Winston Churchill

Never put off until tomorrow what you can do the day after tomorrow.
Mark Twain

Tomorrow is the most important thing in life. Comes to us at midnight very clean. It's perfect when it arrives and it puts itself in our hands. It hopes we've learned something from yesterday.
John Wayne

If men knew how women pass their time when they are alone, they'd never marry.
O. Henry, aka William Sidney Porter (1862-1910), US short story writer, *The Four Million Memoirs of a Yellow Dog*, 1906

Time wounds all heels.
Jane Ace (1905-1974), American radio personality

T R U T H

I made him swear he'd always tell me nothing but the truth. I promised him I never would resent it. No matter how unbearable, how harsh, how cruel. How come he thought I meant it?
Judith Viorst, 1976

Drinking when we are not thirsty and making love all year round, madam; that is all there is to distinguish us from other animals.
Beaumarchais (1732-1799), French dramatist, *Le Mariage de Figaro*

Women are much more like each other than men:
They have, in truth, but two passions, vanity and
love; these are their universal characteristics.
Earl of Chesterfield (1694-1733), English statesman,
letter to his son, 1749

Unfortunately, sometimes people don't hear you
until you scream.
Stephanie Powers, American actress

U N D I E S

Brevity is the soul of lingerie.
Dorothy Parker

As an article of dress for a girl, the corset must be
looked upon as distinctly prejudicial to health, and
as entirely unnecessary.
Howard A. Kelly, US gynaecologist, *Medical
Gynaecology,* 1909

I don't wear knickers – I hate them.
Joanna Lumley, British actress

Taking off my stays at the end of the day makes
me happier than anything I know.
Joyce Grenfell (1910-1980), British actress

V A N I T Y

All politicians have vanity. Some wear it more
gently than others.
David Steel, British politician

I have little patience with anyone who is not self-
satisfied. I am always pleased to see my friends,
happy to be with my wife and family, but the high
spot of every day is when I first catch a glimpse of
myself in the shaving mirror.
Robert Morley

Never underestimate a man who over-estimates
himself.
Franklin D. Roosevelt, on General Douglas MacArthur

Should you be a teenager blessed with uncommon good looks, document this state of affairs by the taking of photographs. It is the only way anyone will ever believe you in years to come.
Fran Lebowitz, Tips for Teens, Social Studies, 1981

I have often wished I had time to cultivate modesty . . . But I am too busy thinking about myself.
Edith Sitwell (1887-1964), English writer

VEGETARIANISM

Vegetarians have wicked, shifty eyes and laugh in a cold, calculating manner. They pinch little children, steal stamps, drink water, favour beards.
J. B. Morton, British writer

I'm very fond of pigs; but I don't find it difficult to eat them.
Robert Runcie, Archbishop of Canterbury

The first time I tried organic wheat bread, I thought I was chewing on roofing material.
Robin Williams

VICES

What maintains one vice would bring up two children.
Benjamin Franklin

It seems impossible to root out an Englishman's mind the notion that vice is delightful, and that abstention from it is privation
George Bernard Shaw

Vice is a creature of such hideous mien that the more you see it the better you like it.
Finley Peter Dunne (1876-1936), American humorist

How like herrings and onions our vices are in the morning after we have committed them.
S. T. Coleridge (1772-1834)

Society punishes not the vices of its members, but their detection.
Countess of Blessington (1789-1849), novelist

The closer you get to vice, the less gilt and glamour you find there is to it.
Sophie Tucker (1884-1966)

Some people with great virtues are disagreeable, while others with great vices are delightful.
François, duc de La Rochefoucauld (1613-1680)

If you resolve to give up smoking, drinking and loving, you don't actually live longer: it just seems longer.
Clement Freud

Charity hotline asks children to betray their parents' vices.
A charity has set up a confidential hotline for children to inform on parents who take drugs or drink too much

My secret vice is a massage, I lie back and feel all the stress fade away.
Jacqueline Gold, managing director, *Ann Summers*

I suppose my vice is the fact that I can never do anything by half. That's probably because I'm a Leo.
Ulrika Jonsson, TV presenter

I don't smoke or drink, but I do like women. Is that a vice? And I can't resist lamb chops – with the fat on.
Derrick Evans, aka Mr Motivator, fitness expect

VIRGINITY

I was thinking as I was writing this book, about when Margaret Thatcher lost her virginity . . . or indeed, if she ever did.
Baroness Barbara Castle, promoting her memoirs

It's just awesome to be a virgin.
Youth from Texas, after taking the pledge of sexual
abstinence. The national Chastity Association was launched
to promote chastity before marriage

A simple maid in her flower
Is worth a hundred coats-of-arms.
Alfred Lord Tennyson, Lady Clara Vere de Vere, 1833

V I R I L I T Y

Modern man isn't as virile as he used to be.
Instead of making things happen, he waits for
things to happen to him. He goes with the current.
Something . . . has led him to stop swimming
upstream.
Marcello Mastroianni, Italian actor

V I R T U E

By virtue we merely mean the avoidance of the
vices that do not attract us.
Robert Lynd (1879-1949), Anglo-Irish essayist, journalist

Moderation is a virtue only in those who are
thought to have an alternative.
Henry Kissinger

I attribute that failure to my virtues.
Alan Clark, MP, why he never made it into the Cabinet

Assume a virtue, if you have it not.
William Shakespeare, Hamlet

It is one of the superstitions of the human mind to
have imagined that virginity could be a virtue.
Voltaire (1694-1778), French writer, *Notebooks*

Most men admire
Virtue, who follow not her lore.
John Milton, Paradise Regained

Righteous people terrify me . . . virtue is its own
punishment.
Aneurin Bevan (attrib.)

What, after all, is a halo? It's only one more thing to keep clean.
Christopher Fry, *The Lady's Not for Burning,* 1948

Be virtuous and you will be eccentric.
Mark Twain

What is virtue but the Trade Unionism of the married?
Don Juan, in *Man and Superman,* by
George Bernard Shaw

When men grow virtuous in their old age, they only make a sacrifice to God to the devil's leavings.
Alexander Pope (1688-1744), British poet, *Thoughts on Various Subjects*

Men are virtuous because women are; women are virtuous from necessity.
Ed Howe (1873-1937), American journalist and novelist

There are few good women who do not tire of their role.
François, duc de La Rochefoucauld

Punctuality is the virtue of the bored.
Evelyn Waugh (1903-66), British novelist, *Irregular Notes,* diaries March, 1962

Most usually our virtues are only vices in disguise.
François, duc de la Rochefoucauld, *Maximes*

V I T R I O L

Do they merit vitriol, even a drop of it? Yes, because they corrupt the young, persuading them that the mature world which produced Beethoven and Schweitzer, sets an even higher value on the transient anodynes of youth than does youth itself. They are the Hollow Men. They are electronic lice.
Anthony Burgess, speaking of disc jockeys, *Punch,* 1967

'Surviving at the Top' – the book's title alone . . . is
so perversely marvellous that there ought to be a
contest to invent others that could equal it . . .
Marie Antionette's 'Keeping My Head', Achilles'
'Recovering from a Tendon Injury', Gen. Custer's
'Outfoxing the Enemy', and Jean-Claud Duvalier's
'President for Life.'
John Rothschild, on Donald Trump's autobiography

You lived to tell the tale, did you?
The Prince of Wales, on a visit to a housing project in
East London, to a young mother who told him that she
had met Diana

VULGARITY

Interviewer: You've been accused of vulgarity.
Brooks: Bullshit!
Mel Brooks

Vulgarity is the garlic in the salad of taste.
Cyril Connolly (1903-1974), British critic

Vulgarity is simply the conduct of other people.
Oscar Wilde

Good taste and humour . . . are a contradiction in
terms, like a chaste whore.
Malcolm Muggeridge (1903-1990)

WEATHER

Do not, on a rainy day, ask your child what he
feels like doing because I assure you that what he
feels like doing, you won't feel like watching.
Fran Lebowitz, American writer

The way I see it, if you want the rainbow, you
gotta put up with the rain.
Dolly Parton, American singer and actress

WILLY

He is proud that he has the biggest brain of all the primates, but he attempts to conceal that he also has the biggest penis.
Desmond Morris

A man is two people, himself and his cock. A man always takes his friend to the party. Of the two, the friend is the nicer, being more able to show his feelings.
Beryl Bainbridge, English novelist

I wonder why men get serious at all. They have this delicate long thing hanging outside their bodies which goes up and down by its own will. If I were a man I would always be laughing at myself.
Yoko Ono

. . . He put it back into his pants as if he were folding a dead octopus tentacle into his shorts.
Richard Brautigan

When his cock wouldn't 'stand up he blew his head off. He sold himself a line of bullshit and he bought it.
Germaine Greer, Australian feminist, on Ernest Hemingway

An erection at will is the moral equivalent of a valid credit card.
Alex Comfort, British sexologist

An erection is a mysterious thing. There's always that fear, each time one goes, that you won't be seeing it again.
Kirk Douglas, American actor, in his autobiography, *The Ragman's Son*

I had a good eight inches last night.
Ulrika Jonsson, TV weather girl, talking about the overnight snowfalls

Personally, I've got a very fine five-inch.
Patrick Moore, astronomer

She's a ball-buster. Protect me from her.
Nick Nolte, American actor, of Barbra Streisand

I never trust a man unless I've got his pecker in my pocket.
Lyndon B. Johnson

W I N E

One of the disadvantages of wine is that it makes a man mistake words for thoughts.
Dr Samuel Johnson

'Bucks Fizz' – The orange improves the champagne. The champagne definitely improves the orange.
Prince Philip, Duke of Edinburgh

The point about white Burgundies is that I hate them myself – so closely resembling a blend of cold chalk soup and alum cordial with an additive or two to bring it to the colour of children's pee.
Kingsley Amis, British writer, *The Green Man*

Give me eighteen bowls of wine. Behold, I love drunkenness.
Egyptian female courtier, 17th. Dynast hieroglyphics

It's a naïve domestic Burgundy, without any breeding, but I think you'll be amused by its presumption.
James Thurber, humorous writer

Have a madeira m'dear, it's really much nicer than beer.
Michael Flanders, of singing duo, Flanders and Swan

I prefer the gout.
Lord Derby (1865-1948), British administrator, on trying a South African port recommended for gout sufferers

The Germans are exceedingly fond of Rhine wines; they are put up in tall, slender bottles, and are considered a pleasant beverage. One tells them from vinegar by the label.
Mark Twain, *A Tramp Abroad*

Ah, bottle, my friend, why do you empty yourself?
Molière

Wine makes a man better pleased with himself; I do not say that it makes him more pleasing to others.
Dr Samuel Johnson

And Noah began to be an husbandman, and he planted a vineyard; and he drank of the wine, and was drunken; and was uncovered within his tent.
The Bible, Genesis 9

A man must surely be allowed to take a glass of wine by his own fireside.
Richard Brinsley Sheridan (1751-1816), British dramatist, as he sat in a coffeehouse watching his Drury Lane Theatre burn down

One cup of wine is good for a woman; two are degrading; three make her wanton; four destroy her sense of shame.
The Talmud

W O M E N

Why haven't women got labels on their foreheads saying, 'Danger: Government Health Warning: women can seriously damage your brains, genitals, current account, confidence, razor blades and good standing among your friends.'
Jeffrey Bernard, British columnist

When a man takes an interest in a woman's body she accuses him of only taking an interest in her body, but when he doesn't take an interest in her body she accuses him of taking an interest in someone else's body.
P. J. O'Rourke and John Hughes, Planet of the Living Women, National Lampoon, 1979

Yes . . . very attractive. I never came across any other woman in politics as sexually attractive in terms of eyes, wrists and ankles.
Alan Clark, ex-defence minister, when asked if he found ex-PM Thatcher attractive

Behind every great man is an exhausted woman.
Lady Sam Fairbairn, wife of Tory MP Sir Nicholas Fairbairn

A wife is sought for her virtue, a concubine for her beauty.
Chinese proverb

She is a lady short on looks, absolutely deprived of any dress sense, has a figure like a Jurassic monster, is very greedy when it comes to loot, no tact and wants to upstage everyone else.
I cannot think of anybody else I would sooner *not* appoint to this post than the Duchess of York.
Sir Nicholas Fairbairn, MP, following revelations that the Foreign Office along with the Palace were blocking the move to appoint the Duchess of York as U.N. Ambassador

Women should be in the kitchen, the discotheque and the boutique, but not in football.
Ron Atkinson

Woman begins by resisting a man's advances and ends by blocking his retreat.
Oscar Wilde

WORK

Sitting in an office? I couldn't do it. I've got to be lifting up my frock saying 'Look at this'.
Lindi St Clair, Night and Day

Work is the curse of the drinking classes.
Oscar Wilde (attrib.)

Work is much more fun than fun.
Noel Coward

Work expands so as to fill the time available for its completion.
C. Northcote Parkinson, Parkinson's Law, 1957

One of the symptoms of an approaching nervous breakdown is the belief that one's work is terribly important. If I were a medical man, I should prescribe a holiday to any patient who considered his work important.
Bertrand Russell

Anyone can do any amount of work, provided it isn't the work he is *supposed* to be doing at that moment.
Robert Benchley (1889-1945), American humorous writer

I am a nymphomaniac extrovert; I like sex, I like men, I am a teaser. If you go out, do you enjoy flashing your tits? I do.
Lindi St Clair

Nothing is really work unless you would rather be doing something else.
J. M. Barrie

Some people hate voice-overs. I love them. They're like a haiku poem – you have ten seconds to get it exactly right. Shaving a millimetre or a second off something is riveting.
Joanna Lumley, British actress

When I was young I worked for a capitalist 12 hours a day and I was always tired. Now I work for myself 20 hours a day and I never get tired.
Nikita Khrushchev (1894-1971)

Work is the province of cattle.
Dorothy Parker

There is a time for work. And a time for love. That leaves no other time.
Coco Chanel

The harder I work, the better I feel.
Margaret Thatcher

I would like to take my mother to one side and advise her to cut down her workload, but I know she would take absolutely no notice.
Carol Thatcher, of her mother Margaret Thatcher

XENOPHOBIA

With its open-door immigration policy, the United States is perhaps the only state not afflicted with xenophobia, but the very warp and weave of our national fibre is even now being eaten away by swarms of wops, d.p.s., p.r.s., coons and foreigners generally.
The National Lampoon Encylopaedia of Humor, 1968

Abroad is unutterably bloody and foreigners are fiends.
Nancy Mitford, The Pursuit of Love, 1945

If the French were really intelligent, they'd speak English.
Wilfrid Sheed, Taking Pride in Prejudice

The Italians . . . you can't find one who is honest.
Richard M. Nixon

INDEX